Advance praise for *The First 30 Days*:

"What could you do to start loving your life more? This book helps you answer that question and provides the tools you need to make it happen."

> —Marci Shimoff, *New York Times* bestselling author
> of *Happy for No Reason, Chicken Soup for the
> Women's Soul*™, and featured teacher in *The Secret*

"Ariane has a wonderful, warm, inspiring approach to life, to changes we all go through and to what's important. This book is filled with ways to make change simpler, easier, and less stressful. I highly recommend it."

> —Mike Dooley, author of *Notes from the Universe* and
> featured teacher in *The Secret*

"*The First 30 Days* is ideal for anyone going through a change, wanting to make a change or helping someone through a change. There are gems of wisdom in here that will make a difference in how we all get through change and transitions in life."

> —Karen Salmansohn, bestselling author of
> *How to be Happy, Dammit*

"There is no getting around it: change is waiting for you right around the corner, so you might as well embrace it. Ariane de Bonvoisin shows you how. Practical and inspiring, *The First 30 Days* turns life's changes from a scary movie into a rollicking adventure."

> —Arianna Huffington, editor-in-chief,
> *The Huffington Post*

the first **30** days

the
first 30
days

Your Guide to Any Change

(and Loving Your Life More)

Ariane de Bonvoisin

HarperOne

An Imprint of HarperCollins*Publishers*

HarperOne

THE FIRST 30 DAYS: *Your Guide to Any Change (and Loving Your Life More)*. Copyright © 2008 by Ariane de Bonvoisin. All rights reserved. Printed in the United States of America. No part of this book may be used or reproduced in any manner whatsoever without written permission except in the case of brief quotations embodied in critical articles and reviews. For information address HarperCollins Publishers, 10 East 53rd Street, New York, NY 10022.

HarperCollins books may be purchased for educational, business, or sales promotional use. For information please write: Special Markets Department, HarperCollins Publishers, 10 East 53rd Street, New York, NY 10022.

HarperCollins Web site: http://www.harpercollins.com
HarperCollins®, ■®, and HarperOne™ are
trademarks of HarperCollins Publishers.

FIRST EDITION

Designed by Level C

Library of Congress Cataloging-in-Publication Data
Bonvoisin, Ariane de.
The first 30 days : your guide to any change (and loving your life
more) / Ariane de Bonvoisin. — 1st ed.
p. cm.
1. Life change events——Psychological aspects. 2. Change (Psychology)
I. Title. II. Title: First thirty days.
BF637.L53B66 2008
155.2'4—dc22   2008001723

ISBN 978–0–06–147283–1

08 09 10 11 12 RRD(H) 10 9 8 7 6 5 4 3 2 1

To mom and dad.
Thank you for a beautiful life so full of change.

Contents

The core of man's spirit comes from new experiences.

—Christopher McCandless,
Into the Wild

the first **30** days

Introduction

Change is the law of life.
—John F. Kennedy

What If I Told You . . .

. . . that the change you are currently going through could be a little easier, smoother, and less stressful?

. . . that people who are good at navigating changes have certain things in common?

. . . that there are proven ways to help anyone through change?

. . . that the change you have always wanted to make not only is possible, but can be made with optimism and calmness?

. . . that change can actually help you love your life more?

Would you keep reading?

This book is designed to help you through any life change; no change is too big or too small. This book will radically alter the way you navigate change. And don't worry: despite the title, the book won't take thirty days! You can read it in just a few hours.

By reading *The First 30 Days,* you will learn how to live life as what I call a *change optimist.* You will become part of a group of people who choose to see the positive in any life change. Not only will this mind-set carry you through your current change, but it will make change easier to handle when you inevitably face it in the future.

Most people have been conditioned to believe certain things about change:

Change is hard and is something to be avoided.

Change makes me feel alone; I'm the only one going through it.

Change takes time, energy, and work.

Change is stressful and involves pain.

If this is how you're feeling right now, you're not alone. We live in a world where change has become the one constant. Think about it: Millions of people are in the process of getting divorced or caring for a parent or child who is sick. Millions of others have recently lost a job, are trying to make financial changes, or want to start a new relationship or lose weight. And there are constant changes in politics, the environment, our jobs, technology, the law, our health-care system and treatment options, education, the institution of marriage, and the shape of the family today. There are changes in how we eat, live, buy things, and even communicate with each other. Given all these changes, it's no wonder we cling to anything that appears stable and permanent, and then go through a tough time when that, too, inevitably changes.

For some, however, change triggers a different response, one of optimism and strength. For these people the emotional roller coaster of change can be managed; fear and anxiety are replaced with a new way of thinking; and there's a true sense of the resilience of the spirit. They still find change hard—they are realistic—but they understand that everyone experiences his or her fair share, and, most important, that everyone comes out on the other side.

Even if you're facing an extremely challenging change like the death of a loved one or a devastating health diagnosis, having a new mind-set about change will radically affect the way you live your life. You deserve to feel differently about change. And this book will help you get there. *The First 30 Days* will give you the tools necessary to initiate a change or to embrace a change that has happened to you. You will come out on the other side feeling hopeful, strong, and calm, with renewed optimism about life. This book is based on the knowledge that something good can come from any change.

Why the First Thirty Days?

Several years ago, while attempting to settle into a new job (my seventh in ten years, if you're wondering), I wrote my thoughts in a journal, as I always do. I described my feelings during the first thirty days of this new position. I saw my doubts (*Am I good enough?*), fears (*What if I fail?*), and impatience (*When am I going to feel like I really belong here or be given any real work to do?*). I saw that these were the same feelings I had experienced during the first few weeks of all my previous jobs—which was a strange realization, given that these jobs were in a variety of industries across Europe, Asia, the United States, and even Africa! But it was even stranger to discover that these were the same feelings I had when my last relationship ended and were also what I felt as child when

I had difficulty adjusting to yet another new school. As all of these familiar emotions continued to show up during radically different changes, I also began to see a pattern in what I was doing to get through changes. I became aware of what was making these changes easier to handle and move through.

In examining the changes that I've experienced and that I've seen others go through over the years, I noticed that the first few days and weeks of any transition were often the hardest and most emotional, but also the most exciting and the most important to understand. This is the time when we are least able to think clearly and practically. But if we approach change with a positive mind-set, ask the right questions, use the best tools, have a plan, and surround ourselves with strong, inspiring people, it will no longer seem so daunting and our path so uncertain. People who navigate the first thirty days of change successfully will find that they transition through the rest of their change—and future changes—with more confidence and clarity.

The title *The First 30 Days* is a metaphor to help you get started. This book isn't an exact day-to-day approach for moving through change. If your change began a lot longer than thirty days ago but you're now ready to start accepting, understanding, and moving through it, this is also the right book for you. Don't put off embracing the change that has come into your life or initiating a change that you've always wanted to make. You are in the right place.

How This Book Works

Within *The First 30 Days* you'll find nine principles that will guide you through any life change. These principles will help you understand what's holding you back and will demonstrate how to take action and move forward. However, *The First 30 Days* is *not* a regimented thirty-day action plan that lets you sit back and tells you what to do. It's not a twelve-step approach, either. If any of these did exist, I know one thing for sure: they would change! *The First 30 Days* is about a different way of looking at change; it's about the creation of a new mind-set. Think of it as the ladder you use to climb out of a dark hole or as directions to the light at the end of the tunnel. *The First 30 Days* will guide you toward the positive in every change and will inspire you to love your life even more.

Each chapter of the book opens with a principle about change. We will discuss this principle in detail while introducing you to people who have gone through real-life changes. Each chapter also features action points to help you integrate the change principles into your own life. Moving through change requires action, and this is a place to start.

Finally, each chapter ends with the three most important things to remember—concepts that will help you today and going forward as you begin approaching life with a new foundation and understanding of change.

As you journey through *The First 30 Days,* remember that you are unique and so is the way you move through change. As I always say: you can take the bus, the plane, the train, or a surfboard to get to where you're going. It's not my job to choose for you; only you will know what's right. Parts of the book will feel like they have neon lights above them, the things that really hit home, and others won't resonate as strongly. Some principles may seem obvious, but before you skip over them, ask yourself if you have really integrated them into your life. And sometimes I'll ask you to stretch or even "change" your mind, beliefs, and view of the world.

What You Will Learn

The First 30 Days will put you on the path to becoming a change optimist. You will be able to generate the positive beliefs and self-confidence that are the key components of a successful response to change.

One of the principles that guides this entire book is the belief that from any change, even the most difficult and incomprehensible, something good will come. I call this the *change guarantee*. Every change I have been through, including the really hard ones, have added something to my life. This good thing hasn't always occurred when I wanted it to, or in the way I could have imagined, but it *has* always happened. From a loss, there is always something to be found. One of my favorite sayings is "You cannot see around corners." You just have to keep moving forward, trusting that there's something good around the bend. There is great power in not always knowing why things happen the way they do but in trusting that they're happening exactly as they should and that something positive will reveal itself.

Your new approach to change begins now, but it will continue to carry you beyond the first thirty days and into the future. The wisdom of this book will faithfully accompany you through all of the changes still to come.

And if you need more information, we have more stories, more inspiration, more research, and more experts ready to help you create momentum in any life change at our Web site: www. first30days.com.

Ariane

1

Change Your View of Change

Beliefs Can Make All the Difference

Principle 1: People who successfully navigate change have positive beliefs

Your biggest need right now is to develop new beliefs: about yourself, about this change and about life in general. Nothing will have a bigger impact on the way you move through change.

What you believe about change—and about yourself—will be the major filter for how you get through your current transition, whether you're in day one, day thirty, or years past the start of the change. A belief is something you think is true. It can be very strongly ingrained, like a conviction; or weaker, like something you happen to think is correct. This means that if you believe that change is difficult and terrible, you will likely have a difficult and terrible time. The beliefs you have about who you are also directly affect how you feel during change. Are you strong and capable, or unsure and fearful?

There are some striking differences between people who are good at change and those who struggle. People who embrace change—the people I like to call *change optimists*—think: *Change is good. Change is about growing, and something exciting may be waiting for me on the other side of this transition.* They believe that change brings something new into their lives and that change always serves somehow. When change is thrust upon them or when they need to initiate a change on their own, these optimistic people try to make the best of the situation by looking for the positive.

> *Progress is impossible without change, and those who cannot change their minds, cannot change anything.*
> —George Bernard Shaw

The people I have met who fear change usually believe that change is hard, that it brings up all of their anxieties and insecurities, and that it takes forever. They also think that they are unlucky if tough change comes into their lives, and that they will be paralyzed, stressed, and unable to move past it.

Can you see the difference in these two ways of viewing the world?

Which one sounds familiar to you?

The quickest way to take control during change is first to become aware of what your mind is feeding you and then to make a concerted effort to choose better thoughts and beliefs. Start to notice what you most often think and say to yourself—and to others. For example, if you break up with someone, you may believe you will be single forever because you are not attractive or worthy of a committed partner. If you get sick, you may believe that the illness is permanent and that you will never feel better. If you try to lose weight, you may believe you will fail yet again. And if you lose your home in a hurricane, you may believe you will never be happy or comfortable again. These are all beliefs you have created in your own mind.

The good news is that we can identify and bust the myths and fears we have about change. We have a choice about what things mean to us. We create our distortions and our truths. They are part of the software that runs the computer inside our head. We all have the same hard drive, but each of us has unique programs that control our life. Once we have identified the most dominant programs (beliefs) running on our computer, we have the ability to drag the negative ones into the trash and replace them with programs that will serve us better. We can see this in the person who was fired and quickly moved on to a better job versus the person who wallowed for years in unemployed misery. Or the cancer survivor who used the illness to find a renewed love of life versus the survivor who is still full of fear and uncertainty. The difference between these people is the beliefs that they hold.

The Tribe: The Source of Your Current Beliefs

In a perfect world, our parents would teach us that change is the only guarantee in life and that it is therefore essential to be good at accepting change and moving through it. Wouldn't it have been great if your mom had asked you each evening, "What changed today, what is new, and what's good about that?" Acknowledging changes in this way would have helped us develop a view of change that would support us later in life, when we are faced time and time again with new situations and experiences.

Take a moment to think about why you have made the life choices that you have—whom to marry, what kind of work to pursue, where to live—and you'll see that we are often a walking imprint of the beliefs of our family and friends—what I like to

The Change Manifesto
An Optimist's Beliefs About Change

Change is a good thing.

Change is part of life and happens to everyone.

Change is an opportunity for me to grow.

Change always means that something good is around the corner.

Change brings seeds of new beginnings and different ways of living life.

Change brings new people, new opportunities, and new perspectives.

Change reminds me that I am not in control of many things that happen and reminds me to let go and surrender a little more to life.

Change helps me strengthen my *change muscle*—my self-reliance, inner fortitude, and inner faith that I can handle anything.

continued on next page

call *the tribe*. Sometimes this loyalty to the tribe is conscious; but most often it is unconscious. This loyalty helps us feel connected to the people in our lives on a deeper level. Your tribe has probably helped shape the way you live, but it can also take away your ability to see and choose the best way to move through change. Every member of your tribe has his or her own model of the world and is all too eager to share it with you. Going against your tribe can be uncomfortable and threatening. If your family believes deeply in the institution of marriage, it takes courage to tell them that you choose to believe that divorce can be a good thing. Or maybe you dream of owning your own business, but your

Change allows me to learn or understand something new.

Change reveals another aspect of my personality.

Change is never a punishment; it is always an opportunity to connect with what's inside of me.

Change allows me to choose how I want to react to something that has happened—by accepting it or resisting it.

Change helps me find my higher self—the part of me that is always there, that doesn't change. Life's unpredictability becomes infinitely easier when I connect with that part of myself.

Change wants me to acknowledge it, understand it, embrace it, and then integrate it into my life and identity.

Change is always on my side. It exists to serve me, teach me lessons, and help me embrace life's mysteries.

tribe always encouraged you to maintain a steady job. Who is in your tribe? Ask yourself who still has power and influence over your choices and the changes you want to make.

As a friend of mine, Kathy, once told me, "During change I've found that a lot of people have a tendency to hold on to other people's patterns. People need to look at themselves and ask, 'Who am I as an individual?' not 'Who am I as the daughter of my mother or father, the wife of my husband, or the mother to my kids?'"

Choosing your own way can be extremely liberating, so start taking your power back from the tribe! Give yourself permission to express your own view of losing a job, being in a relationship with someone of a different faith, or moving to a new city. It's your life and your change. You can seize the opportunity to make the change your own and to better your life in the best way you see fit.

You can also influence the way someone else views a change you are going through. When my friend Diane lost a big, important Wall Street job, it was as if her world had come crumbling down around her. She had taken in the belief—from society as well as her friends and family—that her career was what made her a smart, interesting, and worthy person. She described her job loss with such shame and negativity that I found myself reacting with the same energy. I felt really sorry for her and worried about her future. But if she had decided to see the good in this change and said, "This is great! I'm going to spend some more time with my family, catch up on my reading, hit the gym, or volunteer," I would have been happy and admired her. What you choose to believe and relay about your change determines how others will react to you.

You may not have chosen the change that is happening to you, but you do get to choose your beliefs around it. People can develop their own beliefs at any time in life, whether they're young or old, whether they're deep into a change or just beginning a transition. Everything is always up for discussion.

☑ Take Action

Part 1

To get a sense of your current beliefs, fill in the blanks in the following statements. Feel free to use your own words. I provided some examples to get you started.

1. Change is _____ (hard, interesting, a pain in the neck, exciting, overwhelming).

2. I am _____ at change (good, bad, awful).

3. Life is _____ (fair, unfair, tough, beautiful, full of surprises).

4. The purpose of life is to _____ (love, learn, make money).

5. A crisis is a time _____ (to hide and feel sorry for myself, to learn something, to change something).

6. Work is _____ (challenging, difficult, unpredictable).

7. Relationships are _____ (hard work, a source of love and joy, something I'm bad at).

8. Books about change and this kind of content are _____ (helpful, silly, not my thing, informative).

Take a look at your answers, and see what emerges. Ask some of your friends what they believe. The answers to these questions form the very foundation of how you view life and change, and often are reflected in how your life is unfolding.

Part 2

Look at the change you are currently experiencing. Write down your beliefs about this change (for example, "I will never get well," "I will never stop feeling sad," "I don't have what it takes to succeed," "I am not good enough," and so on).

Now imagine that someone gave you a handful of First 30 Days optimism pills (or that you are now sitting with the most optimistic person you know) and that you are ready to choose better beliefs about this change. What would those beliefs be? Write them down.

Today, start implementing the new beliefs you just created. Remember, research has shown that it takes twenty-one to twenty-eight days for something to become a habit, so if you try on a few new beliefs for thirty days, they will eventually become part of you. You can speed up the process by writing them down and reading them one to two times a day. I have mine written on a small laminated card that I carry in my bag so they are available when I am waiting for the subway or in line at the bank. These new beliefs are like new food for your mind. We have been feeding our brains the same junk for years, so when you finally shift your beliefs, don't be discouraged if your mind initially resists. Being consistent in what we believe is given high marks in our society, so if we are seen to change our beliefs, we may worry that it will reflect badly on us. But push through that concern and take your power back: believe what you want, when you want, and change your mind as often as you want. It's your life and your mind; choose the beliefs that serve you at this point in your journey.

Beliefs That Hold You Back: Getting Out of Your Own Way

What slows down or even stops the flow of change? Believing that we know how everything will turn out. Our minds often feed us a view of the future that is dark, and we then become convinced of how things are going to unfold. But change gives us an opportunity to reevaluate our beliefs about life, love, men, women, relationships, death, sickness, money, work, God, children . . . and the list keeps going. Many of us are defined by these beliefs, which is what makes changing them so darned hard. Why would we want to reexamine what we think is true? No one wants to think that divorce may be a better option or that somehow surviving cancer makes you stronger (although that's what I've heard from dozens of people I've met). No one wants to think that taking a job that pays half the salary may actually make you much happier. No one wants to admit that the death of an aging parent was perhaps the most merciful outcome.

We are obsessed with our point of view—addicted to our version of how the world works—and we live as though our truth is the only truth. I know a man, Mark, who absolutely does not believe in prayer. His proof, he says, is that some people pray and get their desired outcomes while others pray and receive nothing in return. Mark is convinced that prayer is something humans invented to feel better. Perhaps he has tried praying and been disappointed in the past, so now his conclusion is that it doesn't work. For anyone. Ever.

Why do we limit ourselves like this? Because we all want certainty; we want to know what is going to happen and when. In fact, most of us are much more interested in creating this security in our lives than in seeking the truth, because seeking the truth often means admitting that we're wrong or that perhaps we don't know the answer. And finding the truth may also require us to then take action or make a tough decision. In order to go through change in a friendlier way, we must be

The truth will set you free. But first, it will piss you off.
—Gloria Steinem

humble and remind ourselves that it's OK not to know how to proceed. Many times our desire for total certainty is what causes us to feel paralyzed. I have heard people say, "But I just don't know what to do now" or "I am scared of making the wrong decision" or "I feel paralyzed and stuck." These feelings show up when the mind is in unfamiliar territory, when we are faced with a new situation. But we can change our view of change by viewing the uncomfortable moments as an opportunity for tremendous transformation.

Beliefs You Have About Yourself

The most difficult beliefs to unhook are those you have about yourself. And they are the beliefs that are most important for you to watch. Your internal dialogue is often incredibly hurtful and disempowering. When you think things like *I'm not smart, I failed last time, I'm too old, I'm too poor,* you are establishing very strong beliefs that determine how you feel about yourself and how you interact with others. You can change your beliefs about relationships, money, career, or any other area of change you're going through, but the changes you make will have no impact unless you also change your beliefs about yourself. During change you always take one thing with you—yourself—so you need to create empowering beliefs about the amazing and beautiful human being that you are. Focus on the best parts of yourself, and leave the mean stuff behind.

> *Life begins at the end of your comfort zone.*
> *—Neale Donald Walsch*

We will talk much more about this in the next chapter, but for now, take a moment to answer these questions:

1. What are the worst things I say about myself, or believe to be true about the person I am?

2. How do I sabotage myself when trying to make or face a change?

3. Even if it's just for thirty days, what better things can I believe? (Always start with the words *I am. . . .*)

For example, my friend's mother used to say, "I'm not smart because I didn't go to college, and I'm not good at managing my money because my husband always took care of our finances." She now says and believes, "I am very smart and often contribute great ideas to all types of situations. I am very intuitive with my money and can make solid financial decisions." By creating such strong beliefs about herself, she has directly influenced her financial success and the job opportunities that now come her way.

> *The greatest discovery of our generation is that human beings can alter their lives by altering their attitudes of mind. As you think, so shall you be.*
> *—William James*

Optimists believe:

I am loved.

I am strong.

I am smart.

I am safe.

I am surrounded by people and things that can help.

I am worthy.

I am protected.

I am a good person.

I am human, I am not perfect, and I can figure out a way.

Changing how you view yourself is the beginning of building a rock-solid foundation that will get you through any change. It's time to turn the "mean voice" off.

When Life Challenges Your Strongest Beliefs

The hardest changes are those that challenge your deepest certainties about a subject or person. But if you look at the list that follows, you'll see that, very often, life will deliver results that are very different from what you have always thought to be true.

- If I am skinny, I must be healthy.

- If I exercise and eat well, I will never get cancer.

- A doctor will cure me.

- Marriage is forever.

- My kids will definitely go to college.

- Divorce is not an option.

- A corporate job is safe and secure.

- Hard work is the only way to make money.

- I will have a baby only when I am married.

- My father would never have an affair.

- My best friend would never break my trust.

- My spouse will always stay in shape.

Take Rosemary. She believed that if her children were educated and raised in a happy Christian home, they would turn out perfectly. By the time they were grown, however, one of them was in jail for drugs, one was separated, two siblings didn't speak to each other, and one had moved far away to teach English in Japan. Those outcomes didn't exactly fit the beliefs Rosemary had for how her kids were going to turn out. At first she took it hard, blaming herself for being a bad mother. And on top of it all, her husband had died of cancer at age forty. Eventually, she was

> *If you want to make God laugh, tell him about your plans.*
> —*Woody Allen*

forced to question her beliefs about what it really means to be a mother. She moved past the blame and the guilt, and gave herself the freedom to accept what she could control and what she could not.

When life turns out differently than you had hoped or planned, it's hard to accept. Not only has something changed on the outside, but often your identity has also changed or been challenged. A change in your identity can sometimes be even harder to get through than an exterior change.

Why are identity changes so hard? They challenge our values. That's why accepting change becomes more of an inward journey into what we choose to believe. And exam-

> *Of the forces which are imperceptible forces, none is greater than that of change . . . all things are ever in the state of change . . . therefore the I of the past is no longer the I of today.*
> —*Chang Tzu (ancient Chinese text)*

ining our beliefs can be difficult, because we crave an action plan based on the practical things to do, not some unclear, internal journey of exploration. As I often say, "The actions are easy; the emotions are hard." A change in your identity can also be a slow process. You don't push a button and then there you are, the new you. But don't forget that this in-between phase of development is also a great place to be: you've left something behind and are now in the space of defining and exploring the next phase of yourself. Be gentle. Give yourself time.

Once you are ready to create a new belief system about change, your first step is to figure out what, exactly, your original beliefs are. The next time a change occurs, look beyond the details of the change and ask yourself what belief of yours is being challenged. For example, if you got fired, the beliefs it may be triggering within you could be any of the following: *I am nobody without a job. People will judge me if I am unemployed. My job is the most im-*

> **There is nothing bad, but thinking makes it so.**
> **—Shakespeare**

portant thing in my life. Working is my safety net. Women won't date me because I don't have a secure job. If you are overweight, you may believe that people will perceive you as less interesting and less intelligent than a thinner person, that nobody will ever find you attractive, or that you are lazy and a disappointment to your family. These beliefs are not based in reality and are nothing more than a creation of your own self-doubt and the influences of your tribe.

Beliefs are hard to reexamine, especially if they have formed part of your identity for years. They form the basis of how you view your experience and what changes you will have the confidence to initiate. Can you see how someone who thinks he is unlucky would be unlikely to see being fired as an opportunity to leave a safe job and start a business? Or how someone who has low self-esteem would find it difficult to initiate and remain on a

The Optimist's Mind-Set
A Different Kind of "What If"

When change makes you mad, sad, stressed, angry, or confused, take a moment to think about creating a new ending. You can do this by asking yourself different types of "what if" questions (that is, not the types that ask, *What if I hadn't done this, said this, or been so stupid?*). These should focus on positive outcomes in the future, and will help to rewire your mind, which might still be stuck in the past. Try these questions:

What if I believe things are going to get better?

What if I really don't know how things are supposed to be?

What if life is working on my behalf?

What if the end of this relationship is a good thing and I am being protected from something bad in the future?

What if not getting the job I wanted is much better for me in the long term?

What if I can learn something from a therapist or a self-help book?

What if this crisis is the best wake-up call I ever got?

What if coincidences, signs, and synchronicities are helpful guideposts along the way?

What if there is something I can't yet see or comprehend that would explain why this is happening to me?

weight-loss program? Our beliefs are often what stop us, not a lack of discipline or courage.

Make a decision now to change the beliefs that are holding you hostage, keeping you down. Try to flip these beliefs on their head, just to see how they make you feel. If you find yourself saying things like "Change is hard," "Life is tough," "I'm just so unlucky," "Men don't like women like me," or "I'm too old to take care of myself," practice telling yourself things like "Change is a good thing," "Life is full of surprises," "I'm lucky," "Men are attracted to all kinds of women," and "I can stay fit and healthy." Whatever negative phrase you say, take a moment to turn it around to the positive.

Change tends to break us open for a short while, making anything seem possible. The first thirty days are the right time to explore new things, to break away from the person we have always been, and to become the person we've always wanted to be.

Being Open-Minded

Open-mindedness is another quality of change optimists.

I recently met a doctor in Chicago who admitted that after over forty years of practice, he now realized how closed he had been to new medical ideas and alternative therapies. Now that he was sick and needing medical attention, he saw the value of these types of remedies.

Being open-minded helps to release the tight grip you have on your established beliefs, and it's also one of the most attractive features you can have as a person. This is the time to stretch your comfort zone. What area of your life do you need to be more open-minded about? Maybe you start believing you can treat an illness with better nutrition and alternative medicine. Maybe you start believing you can learn to paint at age sixty. Or maybe you actually start believing you can find true love regardless of your weight or age—which you absolutely can.

People are drawn to those who are willing to consider something new, who aren't fixed in a point of view. Being open-minded means you don't always need to be right. It means you don't feel weak because you don't know the answer or because you don't have a firm opinion. When you're open-minded, you never know what you might learn. You are open to new ideas, to new beliefs, to trying new things, and to the mystery of life unfolding. And you are open to asking for help.

Change teaches us to think differently about a situation and to see it with new eyes, pointing the camera at a different angle so that we may experience life in a new way—our *own* way. When you suspend your analysis of a change, you give it the space to play itself out in a number of ways. For example, having a broken leg may initially seem terrible, but maybe it's actually a good thing: maybe you will learn about yourself and your body during the healing process, and maybe you'll meet someone important during your hospital stay and physical-therapy appointments. You never know what change will bring.

> *You see everything is about belief, whatever we believe rules our existence, rules our life.*
> **—Don Miguel Ruiz**

✓ Take Action

1. What is the one new thing you need to believe to get through the change you're experiencing or initiating? Write it somewhere where it will be easily visible. If you want more than one thing to believe, go ahead! Start with the following.

   I am . . .

   God will . . .

Life is . . .

This is . . . .

2. What are the strongest empowering beliefs you can have that will help you through any change? For example, when I'm going through change, some of my beliefs are as follows.

This too shall pass.

Things always work out in the end.

I will get through this.

Life is on my side.

I will find a way through.

I'm not alone.

I *can* change.

3. What are the best things you believe about yourself? Your skills, talents, qualities. . . . What makes you, you? Write these down.

4. Think of a few of your best friends—people you admire, respect, and love. Write down their names and their strongest beliefs. (If you don't know what their beliefs are, ask them.) Do any of them hold a belief you would like to try on for a while?

The First 30 Days: What to Remember

1. Beliefs are your blueprint for going through change. Identify which ones help you and which ones don't.

2. Responding successfully to change requires creating positive beliefs about change. (Take some time to copy or memorize the Change Manifesto.)

3. Developing new beliefs takes practice. You are retraining your brain and creating a new habit. Pick three new beliefs that represent your new perspective. Soon the beliefs will become more familiar, and eventually they will become automatic. Within a few weeks, you will feel better about getting through this change.

> *You cannot solve a problem with the same mind that created it.*
> *—Albert Einstein*

 # The Change Guarantee

From This Situation,
Something Good Will Come

Principle 2: People who successfully navigate change know that change always brings something positive into their lives.

Every change has a gift associated with it. While it's natural to find change hard, it's important to remember that there are two sides to every coin and that something positive will always come. This is by far the most important belief to have during the first thirty days of change.

I often ask people, "What is the most difficult change you've been through, and what positive thing came from it?" I've heard people say: *I was fired and unemployed for months before finding a new and rewarding career that I now love. I got divorced, never believed I would meet another woman, and am now in a loving relationship. I moved to a city where I knew no one and found my independence as well as the drive to finally pursue my dream of becoming a photographer. I had a heart attack and changed the way I eat and exercise for good. I was submerged in debt and finally learned how to manage my finances. I lost a parent and am now closer with the rest of my family and more motivated to live a fulfilling life.* The change optimist knows that from each story of change, something positive is born. It may be as simple as learning something about yourself, discovering a new friend, or reconnecting with your family.

Even the hardest, most painful changes will eventually bring a gift to your life. Sometimes it will be obvious; at other times it will take a while to realize. But no matter what, change will always lead you to something good. Take comfort in knowing that if you are in an uncomfortable situation, it will change for the better. In any case, it *must* change to comply with the Law of Change. The Law of Change states that all things are constantly in a state of flux; so nothing is permanent, including difficult times and situations. They, too, will pass. As author John A. Simone, Sr. said, "If you're in a bad situation, don't worry it will change and if you're in a good situation, don't worry it will change!"

> **Hidden in any misfortune is good fortune.**
> —Tao Te Ching, *verse 58*

For me, the mind-set of radical optimism—and looking for the positive—began at home, in an unpredictable way. On the outside it looked like I had a wonderful, exciting childhood. I grew up in five countries on three continents, was exposed to different cultures and religions, and even picked up a few languages along the way. Change was the constant in our house—new schools, new friends, new environments. But on the inside, behind closed doors, things were not so bright. My parents' marriage was very difficult. They had no real love or affection for each other, although they did their best to be good parents. My brothers and I lived through some happy and some tough moments. From the age of twelve, I encouraged my mother to get divorced. This period was as hard for my parents as it was for us. My mother's weight would soar, while my father would fall into bouts of anger and stress. And I was often the one who would try to stop their fights, consoling my mother and attempting to be perfect for my father. I saw that my mom felt trapped by her financial dependence on my father, and I watched as our family's lack of honest communication created deep chasms between all of us. My parents finally got divorced, after thirty years in a marriage that was unhappy for everyone involved.

How did my parents' divorce turn me into an optimist? What good could possibly have come from all of this? My mom eventually lost weight, cured her depression, and was hired for several interior-design jobs, which allowed her to do something she had always wanted to pursue. Now she also takes care of two orphaned kids and finds time to travel all over the world. She even added a marathon to her list of accomplishments; she ran one with me when she was sixty! Most important, my mom has developed one of the most positive, "Things always work out" attitudes. She wakes up happy, in love with life, and is spontaneous and grateful. As for my dad, he is calmer, very present in my life, a loving grandfather, and has a healthy relationship with a new woman. He now works with charities and is amicable to my mother when they see each other. He and I even went away on holiday together for the first time this year.

And for me, the list of good that came from this change is endless: it helped me forgive my parents and understand that I also have the ability to forgive anyone. It inspired me to seek out teachers who helped me process the difficult things I had witnessed growing up and to make healthy choices for my own life. I picked up my first self-help books when I was barely sixteen and found my spiritual path very early. My parents' divorce also taught me that it is OK to be both strong *and* vulnerable; I learned to choose men who have a deep ability both to love and to express emotion. I also became financially independent at a young age after seeing my mother suffer from having no money of her own. Most important, all of the changes I experienced when I was young, the exciting ones and the difficult ones, helped me get better at living through change, so that one day I would have the honor and privilege of helping others with the changes in their lives.

Answering the Biggest Questions

While going through change, we often zoom in on a few questions: *Why did this happen to me? Why do I have to go through this change in the first place? Why is this change so hard?* Even the really good changes are hard. Though I certainly don't have the definitive answer—no one does—your own answer to these questions will make a big difference in the way you view life changes, transitions, decisions, and crises, and how easy or difficult they are for you to move through.

> *When times are good, be happy; but when times are bad, consider: God has made the one as well as the other.*
> *—Ecclesiastes 7:14*

To me, the purpose of change is to learn. No matter what, change always shows me new parts of myself. It refines my spirit and uncovers who I really am. Change makes me a better person. Change helps me accept the life I've been given and the mystery of the journey we're all on. It also shows me that there are aspects of life I can't control, and it helps me trust more. Change prepares me for whatever else may be in store for me and strengthens a muscle— what I call the *change muscle*—that we all need to develop as healthy human beings.

Change means something new, and something new always makes you grow—even if how you grow is not what you expected. So when something changes, imagine that life wants you to grow in some fashion.

- Even when someone dies, something else will be born.
- Even when someone is diagnosed with an illness, something will come from the experience.
- Even when you go bankrupt, something new will happen to your finances.
- Even from the worst divorce, something positive will manifest itself in time.

Another friend of mine, Joseph, takes it one step further. He thinks change exists to help us live, love, laugh, learn, and lighten up more. In his mind, change is an opportunity to do more of these things, not less. However you define change, understanding that it isn't inherently a bad thing—as disruptive as it may feel right now—and believing that something good will come from it will help you move past the period of suffering and uncertainty and on to a brighter future. Something good is always around the corner.

Gary, a close friend, is an example of how hardship, hurt, anguish, and pain from a hard change can still be translated into something positive. At thirty-seven, he had a happy life in Florida. He was making a good living until one day he found himself in the middle of a situation we pray we'll never experience—an experience that led him to the *change guarantee*—the belief that from any change, even the most difficult and incomprehensible, something good will come. He was driving home when a mother started to run across a busy street with her three kids. She panicked at the last moment but told the youngest boy to keep running. Gary didn't see this and accidentally ran over and killed the five-year-old child.

After years of working through extreme guilt and pain, even contemplating suicide, Gary turned his anguish around. He looked for what good could come out of this tragedy and channeled all that he had learned about strength, compassion, and forgiveness into a career that could help others. "The accident set the stage for me to be a completely different person, because I'm nothing at all like I was when it happened," he says. "I believed there was something bigger in it, and I looked for the something bigger. I made this tragedy count." Gary felt obligated to do something meaningful with the change he had lived through and began speaking publicly about his experience. "I now travel all over the world, speaking to thousands of people about forgiveness, fear and sadness, honesty, and gratitude. I want people to love what they see in the mirror despite anything that they may have done or that may have happened to them in the past." Gary, who is now in his mid-sixties, regularly inspires audiences to make changes in their own lives. "What happened to me has given me the opportunity to help thousands deal with grief, shame, and loneliness. It has also given me the opportunity to speak about the power of truth, of integrity, and of character. Not

> *After Divine Chaos, always comes Divine Grace.*
> *—Desiree Marin*

a day goes by that I don't feel the power of that little boy next to me." Gary lives and breathes this First 30 Days mind-set.

Though it may be impossible to believe it while you're in the middle of a transition, change is actually working to put you on the path to learning something important for the next phase of your life. Change can help you get in touch with an emotion you've been suppressing. Change can give you the push or inspiration to finally pursue a dream or to change your lifestyle—perhaps by moving, dating again, quitting smoking, losing weight, or drinking less. And change can open your eyes to a new way thinking and feeling.

Life is Your Partner

When you believe the change guarantee, you acknowledge that the universe is setting you up to succeed, not fail, and change becomes easier. It may not look or feel like it, but change is not here to hurt, anger, or attack you. This shift in perspective is one of the most profound changes you can make in your life. And it's not as hard to accomplish as it seems. Once you've made this adjustment, the world can change around you, but you will be equipped with the necessary resources to confront each new situation.

> *The single most important decision any of us ever have to make is whether or not to believe we will live in a friendly universe.*
> *—Albert Einstein*

When I was going through a difficult breakup, someone said to me, "Imagine you are in Las Vegas and you can choose to put all your money on two bets: either you trust the universe to do what's best for you now, or you don't. Which one do you want to bet on?" Whatever the situation, there is always much, much more to be gained by placing our chips on the universe.

Recently, my handsome friend James was in a bad skiing accident that crushed the entire right side of his face. He had multiple fractures, including two in his eye socket and two in his cheekbone. The doctors told him that it would take six weeks for his bones to heal and that they weren't sure what he would look like afterward. Upon hearing this news, James's first thought was, *That's standard time for standard people thinking standard thoughts,* and he told the doctor, "Thank you, but I'll do it in three weeks." James determination to get well was connected to his belief that this change, though painful, would ultimately bring good into his life. "I knew everything happened for a reason and was looking for the positive here as hard as I could, wondering what life wanted me to learn this time. I had been working really hard on a big project for the last year and neglecting other parts of my life. I guess this was a way of slowing me down when I wasn't listening to the little hints." Through a nonstop sense of humor—he even joked in the ambulance on the way to the hospital—and bright outlook, James embraced the change guarantee.

> *Have great faith in yourself—with every ounce of effort you make, you have an immense amount of grace supporting you. Grace is with you every step of the way on this journey.*
> —Gurumayi Chidvilasananda

"The challenge most injured people face is that in the absence of finding a positive meaning in their situation, they start to resent their affliction rather than viewing it as an opportunity—an opportunity to change the pace of their lifestyle, to appreciate the health they may have previously taken for granted, and to meet new people who help them along the journey," James says. "Personally, my injury also gave me the time and perspective in my hospital bed to see that the woman I was with at the time was not who I wanted to marry and enabled me to go and spend quality time with my father, who wasn't well." He got out of the hospital with a few iron screws in his face and still had his rock-solid outlook.

Like James, when going through change, especially the hard ones, I immediately start looking for the good, and in doing so I encourage something positive to come to me. What you put out will come back to you. Yes, it's important to be patient: the good that comes from change doesn't always reveal itself quickly. But people who believe that good things will come are the ones to whom good things happen. Believe that the only reason change happens is to make your life better, and your life will be better.

Here are some examples from my own life that show that from change something good will always come. (Keep in mind that some of the good things may seem really small and unimportant at first, but that's how you start.)

I didn't get into my top choice of college, but . . . *I had the greatest time at the college I ended up at. It was no doubt the perfect place for me and today I don't regret it at all.*

I was unable to hire my first choice for a big job at my company, but . . . *I found someone better suited for the position in a matter of weeks.*

I missed my flight home on a recent trip when I really needed to get back quickly, but . . . *I met two great people at the airport who have become good friends.*

I was dumped by someone I was really excited about, but . . . *I soon saw that he wasn't someone I wanted to be with in the long run.*

I didn't go through with my engagement, but . . . *I now choose men with a commitment to spiritual and personal development, which is essential for me.*

For the two years it took to get my company funded, I lived without a salary, but . . . *being patient led me to the perfect investors and the right people to help me make the company the best it can be.*

I lost a big, important deal, but . . . *I realized that the people slated to be my future business partners were not people I could really trust or even enjoyed working with.*

It took me a few years to lose some extra weight and finally be happy with how I look, but . . . *the weight has stayed off because I lost it the healthier way, by eating right and exercising.*

I was not attractive or popular as a teenager, but . . . *today I relate to everyone, no matter how they look or feel.*

> **The Spanish have a lovely phrase, "No hay mal que por bien no venga," which, when translated into English, means, "There is nothing bad that isn't followed by something good."**

I once experienced a really tough change with my finances. During the Internet boom, I invested all of my hard-earned savings in the stock market because everyone seemed to be making a fortune. By the age of twenty-eight I had made more money than I ever expected. I was ecstatic at the thought of such great financial security. Then my broker started making some very risky trades, and although my intuition told me daily that something was wrong, I believed he had the experience that I didn't, so I let him proceed. What resulted was devastating. I lost it all in a matter of weeks. This was money I had planned to use later in life to start a business, to help my mother, to buy myself some freedom. I beat myself up for not listening to my gut about the broker and his strategies. I hated myself for having been irresponsible.

It took me a while to even consider that something good would come from this drama. I tried to get the money back, and I worked hard to forgive, to not focus on the past. Today, I can say that I am much smarter financially. I understand that money is not a game, I always trust my intuition, and I am a better investor. And I found the drive to build a company that I hope will really make a difference in people's lives. If that weren't enough of a change guarantee, I also met a wonderful broker in a new firm who has been like family to me, and I was able to forgive the broker who lost everything. Overall, the experience taught me to trust my intuition no matter what, that I have the ability to move through anything life may throw at me, and that something good *always* comes from change.

✓ Take Action

1. Now it's your turn to identify tough changes you've gone through and the good that ultimately came from them. If you can't identify the good that has come, write down what could be a good thing at some point in the future. (Force your brain to do this even though it will kick up a fight.)

2. Identify the changes you are struggling with now, and imagine the good that could come from them. See yourself in a year or so, and picture the best outcome that could come from what is happening today. There is nothing wrong or disrespectful in looking for something positive. Healing does not mean forgetting. It means moving forward with what happened. Remember, you get what you focus on, so the sooner you focus on why something might be a good thing or how you can use this

change to do something positive, the quicker you will move toward making the object of your focus a reality.

When you are going through change, what are the advantages that life may be bringing you? What is the good that may come?

- New possibilities and new choices in a specific area

- New people in your life

- Realizing you are strong and can handle anything life throws at you

- Increased adaptability

- Strengthening of your faith

- Healing (physically and emotionally)

- Moving closer to what you really want out of life

- Great lessons and wisdom

- A new idea to pursue

- Increased awareness

- Better understanding of who you really are

- Realization of dreams and desires

- Less fear

Change: Not a Logical Equation

Sometimes the good that comes from change is in no way related to what you have gone through. You may work through a painful breakup only to find that a few months later you get your dream job in another city. Or after your company goes bankrupt you find the time to go back to school to prepare for the career you've always wanted. Or your offer on a house is rejected, but in a few months you meet someone and move into his or her place. Or you are on your way to divorce court when you overhear two men talking about great stock tips, which subsequently make you a fortune. Always be on the lookout for good changes, and not necessarily in the area of your life where you expect to find them. The optimist knows that with time and a little perspective, the pieces of the puzzle always fit together, make sense, and bring something positive into his or her life. All things work together for good.

This was certainly true for Pam. She lost her father when she was only twenty-six, and his death gave her firsthand experience of the change guarantee. After his death, Pam was devastated and angry at the world. She felt she was never given a chance to really know her father as an adult and was heartbroken that he would never see her get married. But at the funeral, she met—for the first time—family

> *The world hates change, yet it is the only thing that has brought progress.*
> —Charles Kettering

members who were part of her father's Chinese heritage. After connecting with these people, she decided to go on a quest to find the part of her that was missing. She eventually found her grandmother in Beijing and discovered relatives all over Asia she had never known. Finding these people and hearing their stories about her family made her feel whole again, and she went on to fall in love there. Pam felt complete with both her Western and Asian parts integrated, and even started using her Chinese name, which she never used as a child. And after she returned home, the man she had met in Asia became her husband.

Change doesn't have to be hard to fulfill the change guarantee. Any change you have the courage to make or to face will also bring something good.

Extensive research has shown that people who have gone through all types of changes feel they have received something in return. They

- recognize their strength;

- are able to handle difficulties;

- have greater appreciation of life;

- have a greater feeling of self-reliance;

- are equipped to accept things;

- reevaluate their priorities;

- put more effort into relationships;

- feel more compassion;

- count more on people;

- develop new interests;

- feel close to others;

- are more willing to express emotions;

- have more faith.

> *The measure of mental health is the*
> *disposition to find good everywhere.*
> *—Ralph Waldo Emerson*

The Optimist's Mind-Set:
Think Abundance, and Make Room for the New

When we're faced with a change or contemplate making one, we are programmed to think of scarcity first: There won't be another job, another lover, more money, more happiness, or we won't be able to quit smoking or leave an abusive relationship. We don't remember that the universe is abundant: more is always coming. You are always heading toward something better whether you realize it or not. A different relationship will come along, a better job, or a new opportunity.

I am not asking you to completely change your way of thinking overnight, but try turning to the positive instead of the negative for a little while. Now is the time to activate your imagination and fill the empty space created by change with what you want out of life. An anonymous source said, "Reality can be beaten with enough imagination."

Focus on a positive view of change every day for the next thirty days. Visualize the good things you want in your life, imagine them, give them shape and depth with pictures and feelings.

Changes can be like cleaning house, dusting off the cobwebs and moving around the furniture: The old must be disposed of to make room for the new. All this movement can stir up

> *The great successful men of the world have used their imagination . . . they think ahead and create their mental picture in all its details, filling in here, adding a little there, altering this a bit and that a bit, but steadily building, steadily building.*
> *—Robert Collier*

uncomfortable feelings, but they are temporary. It can be difficult to remember this while deep in change; we may feel like the challenging feelings are permanent because we can't see exactly where they will end. So, while we are experiencing a transition, we would do well to remember that nothing bad ever happens without an equal or greater benefit coming in return. Power comes in believing this, even *before* we know what it is that life has been preparing us for. Jackie Kennedy believed that "a terrible winter would somehow yield to a glorious springtime."

Ask yourself: *What is something I need to get rid of to make room for the new?* Is it a job you hate? A person who isn't right for you? A person you need to forgive? A burden of guilt or anger you carry toward someone? Some extra weight that is making your body less healthy? Clutter in your house? A damaging habit?

What is in your way?

✓ Take Action

Write out these words: *From this situation, something good will come.* Place this phrase in key places around your home and work area. I have positioned this reminder on my fridge, by my bed, and on my computer screen. This way, whenever I receive disturbing news, hear of a change, or realize that something is going in a different direction than I expected, I immediately see the phrase. It's now hardwired into my brain.

The words were given to me by my friend Ismail, from Uganda, who is a wise soul. Although he now lives and works in New York, he spent thirty years in Africa. In his native community, people are unlikely to judge a situation as being anything but good. They believe life is on their side and conspiring to help them always. And that's from people in West Africa—people who you might think have the right to be a bit upset with life sometimes, given the harsh conditions in which they often live.

Understanding the Language of Life

Having faith in the change guarantee is an essential part of what makes someone good at change, but it also helps to get in touch with the invisible realm of coincidences, signs, and synchronicities that surround us. This will help you become more attuned to the positive messages that are right under your nose, messages that life wants you to notice. Even if you think it's random luck, coincidence, or just plain rubbish, try to switch frequencies for a moment or a day, and see whether you can recognize the ways life tries to communicate with you.

- A friend may mention something to you that sparks an idea.

- You may see a billboard that speaks directly to you.

- A movie or television show may offer meaning for you.

- A song on your car radio could remind you of someone.

- An e-mail might cause you to see a connection to what you are going through.

I get signs nearly every day. Recently I hailed a cab to get to a meeting and had three taxis pull up next to me—a nearly impossible occurrence in New York City. I found myself drawn to one cab in particular, and when I got in I found a copy of a *USA Today* article all about Change in America—*Perfect for someone who is committed to building a company that helps people through change,* I thought. My first reaction these days is to laugh at the perfection of it all: this was an important article for me to know about.

Another friend of mine, Bart, experienced the power of coincidence when he made the decision to leave his safe corporate job to begin producing and writing screenplays, a dream of his for years. Soon after he left his position, he found himself stuck in an old belief. He kept telling himself, "I can't write. I'm not creative, I'm a business guy," and he made himself miserable for nearly a year. But then signs began coming in that pointed him in the right direction. "I was introduced to the right business partner, we found an incredible script editor, and we started to notice all these people giving us a piece of the puzzle. That's when it started to become real," he says. "I couldn't have imagined how many coincidences would help along the way, from meeting people who were creatively successful and following their advice to finding surprising financial support. Everything started from taking the initial risk of stepping out on my own, but things really began happening when I allowed myself to notice helpful things all around me and to focus less on my insecurities. Lots of new ideas and opportunities are coming now—none of which I could have predicted three years ago."

> *Change the way you see the storms of your life.*
> *— Wayne Dyer*

So many people complain of unanswered prayers. We are always asking for help to make decisions or to get through change when, really, life is constantly trying to guide us. But life speaks its own language, and it's not one that is taught to us in school. Instead of working to understand what life is telling us, many people prefer to automatically undermine it. Give it a chance. Just for a while. You can help yourself move through change by look-ing for clues to the mystery, for what is next for you, what is around the corner. What thing, class, symbol, book, or person might help you through this change? Visualize yourself with an-tennae on your head. Tune in and start waking up.

Next time you're face to face with change, ask yourself, *Is this a slap in the face, or could this be a pat on the back?* Life has your best intentions at heart, and all it's asking of you is to look at the other side of the coin.

When change happens—and it *will* happen, you know this by now—stand up confidently and say yes to this new phase of your life, even if it's the hardest thing you've ever gone through. Doing so doesn't take away or minimize the life you have lived up until now. It makes you a person who doesn't have to stay in the dark-ness, who can choose to go toward the light, toward hope, toward making a change that will benefit your life. Optimism can be at the center of all that you do and all that happens to you, no matter how difficult or inexplicable a change may be.

The First 30 Days: What to Remember

1. Trust that there is a gift in this change and that life is on your side. Ask yourself what could be good about this change. These types of positive thoughts will help you suc-cessfully embrace change.

2. In the middle of change, become comfortable with the un-certainty of the temporary in-between period. Stay open to

the mystery of what is around the corner, and look for signs that will point you in the right direction.

3. The choices you make create change and determine how easy or hard it will be. Choose to think of abundance—as opposed to scarcity. Choose to believe in hope and optimism. Find an appreciation of life and of yourself in the first thirty days, and you will make your journey through change easier.

> *Amidst the worldly comings and goings,*
> *observe how endings become beginnings.*
> *—Tao Te Ching, verse 16*

3 The Change Muscle

You're Stronger Than You Think

Principle 3: People who successfully navigate change know they are resilient, strong, and capable of getting through anything.

You are much stronger, much smarter, and much more intuitive than you have ever been told. You are more resilient and more powerful. Once you truly know and believe this, you will be able to get through any change—even the hardest one you can imagine.

While we can't deny that change is difficult, we all have the ability to move through it. There is something within every human being that supports us and keeps us alive and moving forward. We are born with a will to survive, a will to get better no matter what, and a will to be happier and feel good again. I have come to refer to this as the *change muscle*. The change muscle is our birthright—there to be used whenever we need it. It's the strength that's in our DNA and the strength that is created from all of the changes that we have been through—the big changes, the small

changes, the unexpected changes, and the changes we have initiated. If you have forgotten about your change muscle, or have yet
to acknowledge it, say hello to it today.

Many times, the actual change is not the real problem. Instead,
we feel frustrated when we can't find meaning in our new situation, when we disconnect from our spiritual side, or when we
struggle with low self-esteem, fear, or a general lack of trust in
where life is taking us. Impatience and a longing for certainty
also get in the way of the natural process of change. But our change
muscle is there to help us adapt and take the action necessary to
move through change.

> *We are all pilgrims on the same
> journey . . . but some pilgrims
> have better road maps.*
> *—Nelson De Mille*

We all know someone who has gone through an amazing life
change. We may have admired his or her ability to stay strong in
the face of great adversity, but what we were actually impressed
with was the magnificent way in which he or she activated the
change muscle—asking body, mind, and soul for every ounce of
strength and courage to move through change. He or she may
have worked through an addiction, left an abusive relationship,
lost a spouse, gotten over a terrible accident, or brought up a disabled child. Think about people you know who fit this picture. If
you can, call one or two of them, acknowledge them and the
change that they've been through, and ask them how they got
through it.

The reality is that we all have this ability. Whatever change
comes into our lives, we can activate the part of ourselves that is
unbelievably strong and will help us move away from a place of
suffering and into a brighter future.

You never know when you will need to activate your change muscle, but you should know that it is always there for you. To make change easier, you need to familiarize yourself with it today. Simply recognizing that this part of you exists is the first step in building a core of strength that is always there, that will help you get through any life change.

I activated my change muscle as I searched for what I really wanted to do with my life. In my twenties, I kept jumping around from job to job, spending about two years at each one. I tried all sorts of things: business, music, TV, the Internet, a nonprofit, and I even went back to graduate school to get an MBA. I got into some very senior positions at a very young age, but either I had climbed the wrong ladder or it was leaning against the wrong wall. I was envious of people who seemed to be living their dream. I would look at them and think, *Wow, they really know what they love, and they've had the courage to do it.* I waited for the day when my calling would finally "hit" me.

Even though I had achieved a fair amount in the eyes of the world, I wasn't happy. I wanted to do something that made a difference in the world. I wanted to feel free, creative, and involved in something that I loved. So, after much stress and deliberation, I began the journey to honestly tell my friends, my family, and myself that the seemingly perfect life I was living was not one that was truly right for me. I had to undo years of learning to see another path, another definition of what success was. I learned that sometimes you need to give yourself permission to do something different, something unexpected, something that might be judged unfavorably—even by people you love. Learning these things played a key role in the strengthening of my change muscle.

I forced myself to make some pretty big changes. First, I left the safety, security, prestige—and paycheck—of a big corporate job and took some time off. Then I took several years to start my business. Launching your own company may sound glamorous, but for me the reality meant a big shift in how I lived my life. One of the hardest changes was adjusting to having no salary—none, nada, zilch. I knew that this would be a natural part of the process in leaving a full-time corporate position, but I didn't realize just how much I relied on having a steady income—relied on it not only financially, but also psychologically and emotionally—as well as a fancy business card and colleagues. Like a lot of other people, I soon figured out that a reliable influx of money in the bank had made me feel confident and secure.

And I quickly discovered that building a business was anything but easy. I found investors, only to have them pull out right before the deal was signed. I hired employees, only to realize that they were not a right fit for the company. And I chose San Francisco as the ideal location for the company, only to decide, three weeks later, to move back to New York City because that was where I needed to be.

> *You gain strength, courage, and confidence by every experience in which you really stop to look fear in the face.*
> *—Eleanor Roosevelt*

As I worked toward my goal, all of my *change demons,* as I like to call them—fear, doubt, impatience, blame, guilt, and shame—surprised me with their unrelenting determination to make me feel lost and unstable. I wondered whether leaving my job had been the wrong decision. I doubted my ability to get my company off the ground. I was embarrassed that I couldn't launch the company any faster. I compared myself with others who had done things better. And I felt stressed out every time somebody asked me how the company was going: I equated the company's success with my value as a person.

Everyone in my life was quick to offer advice. Friends, family, and colleagues told me what I should—and shouldn't—do. Some told me to give up and go back to corporate life; others suggested that I change the direction of the company or merge with another. Still others told me to move back to Europe! Sometimes I listened. But in the deepest moments of doubt and despair, I saw that I was the only one who could make this situation better, together with something inside of me, my spirit. I recalled all of the tough changes that I had already been through as a child, teenager, and adult, and as I listed them, I quickly saw that I had always managed, survived, and sometimes even thrived during change. Life had never really abandoned me. Help had always come in one form or another. I knew that I had the power to move through this change and on to the next phase of my life. My intuition, guidance, and spiritual beliefs told me to keep going. I believed that I was stronger than this change and that it didn't matter what people thought of me or how long it took me to succeed. With a strong change muscle, I knew I would always be OK.

Meeting Your Change Muscle

During change, most of us feel weak and incapable. We haven't been told that we can get through things, so we automatically assume that we can't. But I'm here to remind you that you're much stronger than you've ever imagined. You've already been through many more changes than you realize, and you've helped hundreds of people through change just by being a friend. You have been exercising your change muscle for your entire life. This muscle has nothing to do with how old, educated, or strong you are; it exists in all of us. The change muscle is you acknowledging your strength—telling yourself, *I know I can get through this.*

The change muscle is the part of you that's activated when you have the courage to initiate a change or to get through a change that life throws at you. It's the part of you that says you're going to be OK, you're going to make it through. When you're still standing, still breathing, and still functioning after a change, you've used your change muscle.

Change optimists don't waste time thinking that life is unfair and that there's nothing they can do when changes occur. Instead, they say, *Life's given me my fair share of changes, no more or less than my neighbor, and there is always something I can do to help myself. I'm going to participate in my own rescue.* As human beings we are born incredibly strong and resilient. Since the beginning of time people have survived wars, natural disasters, famine, and disease. Tapping into this strength means using your change muscle.

Like any muscle, the change muscle is strengthened through consistent use. Every time you are faced with a change and move through it, you are activating this part of yourself. And once activated, the muscle is strengthened for life. You can never lose all that you gained from past changes. And the more you acknowledge and use the muscle, reminding yourself that you have the power to get through anything, the more it's going to serve you. Soon you will become more comfortable with change, accepting that it will inevitably come. And when it does, you won't question your ability to make it through.

When we go through changes—big or small—we tend to forget a lot of fundamental truths. We forget how powerful we are; the source of our true self-worth and self-esteem; our strengths, talents, and gifts; our intuition and inner guidance— even our friends and our faith. When you flex your change muscle, you are tapping into these resources. Remember, a muscle is something that gives you strength. It's the same with the change muscle: it's there to give you strength when you need it most.

How the Change Muscle Works

The Change Muscle Has a Memory

Looking back at how you handled previous changes will help you get through change today. When you were going through a big change—maybe you lost your job, moved across the country, or ended a relationship—what did you do to make the transition easier? Did you seek out help from a friend or support group? Did you meditate or pray? Many times people will forget everything they've learned from a change, but it's important to keep track of all that you've gained so it can be applied to the next change you go through. Many of the things you did during a past change can be used to move through changes you're currently experiencing. This is using your change muscle.

> *Our greatest glory consists, not in never falling, but in rising every time we fall.*
> *—Oliver Goldsmith*

By becoming more aware of the changes you've lived through, you will not only recognize all that you've successfully handled but also become more conscious of who you are at your core. And in doing so you will discover what you can fall back on, what has helped in the past. It's not an exact science, but you will come to see that you've been through many changes before and always found the strength and the answers you needed. You may be experiencing brand-new changes, but you're not using brand-new resources.

Kili Moments

When we haven't gone through a change in a while, or we haven't flexed the muscle on our own accord, we feel weakened by change. Change gets easier the more we live through it. Our brains and bodies remember each time we experience change; we know it didn't kill us, and if we take the time to look back, we'll see that something positive eventually came from it as well. And we have also all lived through a significant change that we thought we would never survive. Recalling that moment in time gives us the strength to get through whatever new change has come our way. I call such moments *Kili moments*.

My Kili moment came to me when I was at eighteen thousand feet on Mount Kilimanjaro, just one night away from making it to the summit. When my friend pulled out of the trip at the last minute, I decided to climb alone with a guide who spoke minimal English, and I was facing intense bouts of loneliness and physical pain. The climb had taken six days and had been unbelievably cold and wet, and at this point—I had been given a faulty tent—I wasn't sure I was going to make it. I thought, *There must be something I can do. I am stronger than these circumstances.* At around eleven that night, completely frozen, I scanned the entire base camp for a solution. I soon spotted a sturdy orange tent and woke the owner. I realize now how absurd it must have sounded, but I told this stranger—a

The Change Muscle Is Always There

Your change muscle is always present, but sometimes you need to kick it into gear, reminding yourself of your strength and refusing to be a victim or find excuses. During these moments you may turn to other means of getting through the changes that come lovely Austrian man—that I needed to get into his sleeping bag to warm up! I'm sure he thought he was experiencing oxygen deprivation, but he opened up his sleeping bag and let me climb in anyway. It had taken me eighteen thousand feet and five days until I said, *Ariane, there's always a way to survive, there's always something you can do, and in this instance you're going to have to ask for help.* The next day my new friend and I summited together. As I stood at the top of this majestic mountain in Africa, I thought of one thing: when things get tough for me—whether it's dealing with the ups and downs of starting a new company or nursing a broken heart—I will look back to this moment, my *Kili moment,* and know that I have the strength to get through anything. I had finally become my own best friend. Only you know how hard your Kili moment was and how much strength it took for you to make it through. Don't allow the passing of time to minimize the significance of those moments.

Every change optimist has a Kili moment. What's yours? It could be when you were bullied in elementary school or when you stared death or disease in the face. Perhaps you had a premature baby who nearly died or you helped a parent through severe Alzheimer's. Find your Kili moment—an experience that pushed you to your limit—then ask yourself what it taught you about yourself. Kili moments are invaluable resources for future changes.

your way. You may rely on food, sex, alcohol, or TV. Be sure to take a moment every day to connect with your change muscle, the part of you that is the strongest and has always been there for you. Talk to it, listen to it, and don't forget just how capable you really are.

The Stacking Effect

Your change muscle is with you when you're born, and it never leaves. In fact, it only gets stronger as you move through more and more changes. This is the stacking effect. Every change you've been through, no matter how small and insignificant it may seem, builds on itself and helps prepare you for anything that comes later in life. A lot of people approach change feeling completely unarmed, unprepared, vulnerable, and exposed. But you have the tools to get through this change. You've done it before, and you can do it again. Don't discount the changes you have already lived through. Give yourself the credit you deserve. Success from previous changes and experiences is your ultimate motivator.

> *What lies behind us and what lies ahead of us are tiny matters compared to what lies within us.*
> *— Henry David Thoreau*

Your Change Muscle Is Designed Just for You

Your change muscle is perfect for you. You may look at a friend and think he or she has a better understanding of what to do during change than you do, but the truth is that if you were to compare your "change résumés," you would see that you have gone through many changes that he or she has never experienced and vice versa. Don't waste valuable energy wishing you had what someone else has. You are just as capable and have just as much courage and risk-taking ability as anyone else.

You are a powerful person, and it's time to use your power to go where you want to go. You are born with your own unique guidance system, your own intuition, and your own ability to decide and to think what you want. You have the change muscle that is absolutely right for you.

Take Action
How Strong Is Your Change Muscle?

Read through the list below, and check off the points you believe you already do.

My change muscle is strengthened when I

- ❏ stay physically healthy, active, and fit;

- ❏ eat well (like any other muscle, the change muscle needs good food and good fuel);

- ❏ maintain optimism and hope, and focus on positive things;

- ❏ always learn new things—continually engaging the brain and body in new activities;

- ❏ become conscious of my belief systems and the language I use;

- ❏ forgive and am grateful and honest;

- ❏ believe in myself, in my ability to change, and in life's determination to bring me good things;

- ❏ grieve any pain or loss associated with a change (I let it out by crying, writing, venting);

- ❏ make firm decisions—remain clear and focused;

- ❏ believe that something bigger—some greater power—is on my side, working on my behalf, giving me even more strength that I can tap into;

❑   am present and accepting of the change by acknowledging what has happened and what actions I need to take to move on to the next phase of my life.

My change muscle is weakened when I

❑   get overwhelmed by the change demons—fear, blame, shame, doubt, guilt, and impatience—as well as by anger and any other disempowering emotion that may show up during change;

❑   criticize myself, creating an immediate separation from my inner source of strength;

❑   am closed minded—having the inability to see other options or possibilities;

❑   refuse to trust that something good will come from this change;

❑   compare myself with other people;

❑   behave in accordance with what the tribe expects of me, not activating my personal power and free will;

❑   isolate myself from sources of help or support;

❑   succumb to the need to know what's next by pushing for answers and meaning right away instead of allowing life to unfold at its own pace;

❑   don't trust my intuition;

❑   am a victim, not taking responsibility for my life;

❑   insist on being right rather than listening to what life is telling me;

❑   isolate myself from my higher self;

❑ spend too much energy dwelling on the past or imagining negative future scenarios.

So, are you doing more to strengthen or weaken your change muscle?

In 2003, Peter stretched his change muscle in an unexpected way when he competed in the Marathon des Sables, in which participants run at least one marathon a day for seven straight days across one of the most inhospitable and unforgiving terrains in the world, the Sahara Desert. On day four of the race, Peter awoke with food poisoning and found it nearly impossible to run for the first four hours of the day. He trudged along slowly, struggling with intense stomach cramps, muscle spasms, and severe exhaustion, and by 8 P.M. he had barely covered 30 miles. After realizing that he had another 20 miles to run and taking stock of his battered body, Peter took off his forty-pound backpack and began to search for the distress flair that would summon the helicopter to take him out of the race. "But as I fumbled through my pack—cold, hungry, and exhausted—something incredible happened. A blind Korean man in his late sixties ran by me, tied at the wrist to his guide. In the middle of this vast wilderness, it was the most incredible sight I had ever seen. All I could think of was that if this man could make it—unable to take comfort in the majesty of the scenery, unable to gauge his foot placement on the rocky and uneven floor, and even unable to take comfort from the encouraging looks in the eyes of the other competitors—I could, too," he says.

Suddenly, Peter felt a surge of energy flooding through his body and a burning desire to know what gave this man the strength, vision, and motivation to tackle such a severe physical challenge.

But in order to find out, he first needed to catch him! He stood up, began to run, and found that it was effortless this time. When he caught up to the Korean man, Peter learned through his translator that the man's brother had passed away from cancer years ago and each year his firm intention was to run this race to raise money for the hospital that had looked after him. His passion gave him the courage to enter, compete, and finish one of the toughest footraces in the world. That was all Peter needed to hear. He ran that day's remaining 20 miles, ran the following day's 26.2, and finished the race the day after.

"It was the biggest lesson of my life and made me realize an important and universal truth: we have so much more inside us than we tell ourselves. The body and mind are so strong, and the key to unlocking our potential is not anything we can see or find in the physical world. It's something that happens in the invisible

Another Muscle

Just as you have a change muscle, you also have a *letting-go muscle.* This is something that helps you let go of a person, a place, a thing, or a situation. When you get married you let go of your single years, and when you move to a new city you let go of the life you had in the old city. All change involves loss to some extent. You can strengthen the letting-go muscle before any big changes even come your way. Practice by giving away an object you really love—your favorite coffee mug, a pair of jeans, a prized piece of jewelry. The more you let go of things, the stronger this muscle will be when you need it most. Letting go allows us to make room for the bigger things that are in store for us.

realm of thought and drive, something bigger that we engage to help us achieve our goals. I found a muscle within me I never knew I had."

The Hardest Changes: Often the Best

Through building my company, I have had the privilege of interviewing hundreds of people, and I always ask them a few of what I call *signature questions*. One of them is "What is the best change you've ever made or had to face, one that really made a big difference in your life?"

When I first started asking this question, I assumed people would speak of getting married, having a baby, buying their first home, or getting their dream job. However, this was rarely the case. Not only were these wonderfully positive changes hardly ever mentioned; what people considered their "best" change was often the hardest and most difficult one they ever faced—the one that was the ultimate trainer of their change muscle. It was as if I had posed a different question and had asked them what their worst change had been. They mentioned getting divorced, becoming sober, receiving a cancer diagnosis, losing a loved one, being fired at the age of fifty, or even going bankrupt!

To this day, I look forward to asking people this simple question, because I know that I will nearly always hear about a change that required great courage, great faith, and great use of their change muscle. Ask yourself, *What's the best change I've ever made or faced?*

☑Take Action
Create Your Change Résumé

This exercise is an important part of the First 30 Days experience. Take ten minutes to review your change history, and you'll soon see that you're much stronger than you ever imagined. Knowing what you've already changed and what you've already survived—and the things that helped during those moments—will help you tackle future changes with ease.

1. To begin, list every major change you have lived through. These can be as obvious as changing schools or losing your virginity, or as serious as overcoming an eating disorder or experiencing the loss of a loved one. Start during your childhood, and work your way into adulthood. Keep in mind that you don't need to have scaled a mountain, run through the desert, or survived a fatal illness to have a strong change muscle. Every life change that you have lived through is exactly right for you and contributes to the strength of your change muscle. Write the changes down in two groups: those that were given to you, and those that you yourself initiated.

   People often think that change is only about death, divorce, marriage, and birth, but there are hundreds of other changes that get overlooked. You may have gone to college, graduated, found a job, and secured a place to live. Or maybe you got a tattoo, changed hairstyles, or moved across the country. You could have found the courage to forgive your dad or apologize to your mom. Or you may have lost a job or a pet or somebody's friendship. These are all valid changes that belong to you. Each one carries wisdom and guidance that can help you get through change today.

When drafting your résumé, don't forget the positive changes—uplifting change activates your change muscle, too—and, especially, the changes that you don't want anyone to know about. (After all, this résumé is for nobody but you.) There are some changes that are very visible in the light, that are an outward part of your identity. But it's also important to acknowledge the changes that are pushed into the dark spaces, the changes you are ashamed of, because they're often the ones that bring the greatest stretch to your change muscle.

2. Under each change, list the good things that eventually came from it: maybe losing a loved one gave you the inspiration and courage to change jobs or pursue a dream. And write down what you learned about yourself during the change.

3. Pick three or four of the most difficult changes you have been through. Ask yourself what you did during each change that helped you through it. What beliefs did you develop? How did you overcome your fears? What information did you take away from the experience? Maybe you discovered that you need to spend several weeks grieving the change before you can attempt to move forward, or perhaps you found that simply talking to a good friend relieved much of your doubt and fear.

4. Now, knowing what it is that helps you specifically during change, ask yourself how you can purposefully use your change muscle to get through the change you're experiencing today. What is the next step you need to take?

5. Give yourself credit for your hard work here. You're already strengthening your change muscle!

An Example: Anne Marie's Change Résumé

Changes I made

I asked my father for forgiveness.

I quit smoking.

I left a corporate job to work for myself.

I became a vegetarian.

I ran a marathon.

I had an abortion.

Changes life gave me

My brother committed suicide.

My best friend died unexpectedly.

I got pregnant twice without wanting to be.

My parents separated.

Good things that came from these changes

I am grateful for every day that I am alive and free.

I now have a life I have created on my own terms.

I am in great health.

I am much closer to my parents.

I trained to be a life coach so I could help people handle tough changes.

I now live in a place that I love.

How Positive Change Strengthens Your Change Muscle

Even something positive, like getting out of debt, can strengthen your change muscle. Once you have moved through the change, you can see that by clearing your debts you accepted the fact that you had financial problems, which helped you move forward instead of remaining stuck in one place. When you accept the reality of where you are now and look clearly toward where you want to be in the future, you activate your change muscle even faster.

Personal strategies and beliefs that helped me through change

I believed that everything was going to be OK.

I took one day at a time.

I asked for help and really leaned on my friends.

I cried.

I wrote things down in a journal.

I ate well and got enough sleep.

I started running.

I prayed.

I trusted myself more than anyone else.

I chose to not be a victim or to blame.

I allowed life to unfold and gave up control.

I focused on what small actions I could take to make things better.

At the age of thirty-two Ally was diagnosed with a brain tumor, which put her on a direct path to meeting her change muscle. She underwent two operations, numerous trips to the emergency room, weeks in the intensive-care unit, and weeks in quarantine. Her scalp was shaved, her skin was burned—in a dramatic reaction to a strong antibiotic—and she will live the rest of her life with a hole in her head. But the experience led her to see what good can come from change—the change guarantee—while also giving her change muscle a serious workout. "Throughout the process I got stronger every day. But more than that, I got smarter every day. I slowed down. I saw things more clearly. I breathed deeply. I learned how to be loving and kind again and how to take things lightly. I'm grateful for the experience. Having never valued my life until the time it was about to be taken from me, I found a new appreciation for everyone and everything," she says. "Life will never be the same. It will only be better. It's been thirteen years since that summer, and a day doesn't go by that I don't have some reminder of where I've been. But the ultimate outcome was to find myself a stronger person, feeling capable of overcoming any obstacle." (Ally now works with me at my company.)

Only you know how hard this change is for you today, or has been, or will be, and only you know how much you have to, have had to, or will have to activate your change muscle to get through it. Whenever you feel stuck or overwhelmed, tap into the part of you that is untouchable, calm, and knows what to do next to survive. The change muscle is a tool that is a constant part of you. It is a self-esteem builder, a constant friend, and a source of never-ending strength. As Wayne Dyer says in *Change Your Thoughts, Change Your Life,* "You must understand the great within yourself." Greatness is not found inside of a relationship or a bank account;

it is found inside you. It's not easy to make big changes and activate the change muscle, but it gets easier every time you do.

When you feel weakened or unsettled by a change, remember your muscle. Now that you know it exists, don't push your greatness and inner strength away; they are there to make change easier.

The First 30 Days: What to Remember

- You are much stronger, more resilient, more intuitive, and more resourceful than you think.

- You are born with a change muscle—an innate ability to go through change. You won't feel weak if you remember how strong you really are.

- Your change muscle remembers every change you've been through and every lesson you've learned, and it will help you move through this one. The changes you have experienced in the past will help you adjust to all types of changes in the future.

I can be changed by what happened to me. I refuse to be reduced by it.
—Maya Angelou

Change Demons

*How to Recognize Negative
Emotions and Move Past Them*

Principle 4: People who successfully navigate change know that every challenging emotion they feel is not going to stop them and will guide them to positive emotions that help them feel better.

Negative emotions can stall us, making change harder, while the positive ones can help us move through a change in a simpler, quicker, and more conscious way.

We all have a change we would love to make, and many of us are going through a change right now. Yet we still find it difficult to move forward with courage and optimism because we're held hostage by our negative emotions. These disempowering emotions can wreak havoc on our self-esteem, destroying our hope, making it difficult to take action, and keeping us stuck in the past or unable to see future opportunities. But we are not alone: everyone feels these emotions to some extent.

But here's the good news: these change demons—as I call them—exist to guide us, to show us whether we are heading in the right direction. They can be a positive part of the First 30 Days experience. Any discomfort we feel is here to serve us. Instead of dodging, ignoring, or hiding from these emotions, welcome them, and thank them for showing you the way through change.

Through researching and building the first30days.com Web site, and through my own personal experience with change, I've come to recognize six primary emotions or change demons: fear, doubt, impatience, blame, guilt, and shame.

The change demons have a lot in common:

- They help you figure out how you don't want to feel—and, correspondingly, how you *do* want to feel.

- They are temporary.

- They exist to get you back in alignment with your higher self—the calmer, wiser version of yourself, the part of you that is connected and clear.

- They require you to recognize how you're feeling and to pick preferable emotions to take their place.

- They each come with a twin emotion that will help you feel better.

- The change demons are an essential part of what I call the *change GPS*.

The change demons help us navigate through change by alerting us if we are off course and encouraging us to choose a different emotion to help us get to where we want to go. A GPS asks only two questions: *Where are you now? Where do you want to go?* Or, in emotional terms: *What are you feeling now? What do you want to feel instead?* A navigational GPS system needs you to be very specific about where you want to go, and so does the change GPS. Know where you want to end up, and make that destination clear.

The most important first step is to become aware of these demons, to be able to identify which one is consuming you. Only then will you be able to understand how to move beyond it. Once you have recognized the emotions you are experiencing, you'll come to see that every change demon can be replaced by a corresponding positive emotion—an antidote to the painful feeling—that will lead you from a place of suffering to one of acceptance. Remembering this simple principle can shift feelings of negativity or "stuckness" to feelings of hope and clarity. Though it may not feel like it in the moment, you actually have control over your emotions. Becoming conscious of these change demons—and replacing them with empowering emotions—is sometimes more important than fixing the problem that caused them.

The night before I turned thirty, I ended a serious relationship and was convinced I'd never fall in love again. Determined to live up to the powerful pull of the tribe—I felt that my family, friends, and society at large expected me to be married by the time I was thirty—I made a commitment to myself that I'd be engaged by my next birthday. Little did I know that sometimes you really do get what you wish for. Soon after, I met someone who fit the picture of the guy I was supposed to marry. He was handsome and successful, and he had many of the characteristics I thought I wanted in a man. We dated for six months before I realized that something was off. By this point in my life, I understood that it was essential for my life partner to have a strong sense of spirituality, which was exactly what this man was lacking. But instead of listening to my heart and seeking out the kind of partner my higher self wanted, I made the decision to stay with him from a place of fear. I wanted it to fit. I kept pushing aside my nagging feelings of doubt until finally, after many days and nights of questioning and confusion, I was completely miserable and finally ready to break up with him.

But he had other plans: a surprise trip to Colorado. And while we were away he shocked me even further by proposing on my birthday (exactly a year from when I had made that commitment in my head!). When he asked me to marry him, my first thought was, *Oh no!* But my fears took over. Even though I knew that something fundamental was wrong in our relationship, I was still considering playing it safe and marrying this man. So I said yes.

We went back to our hotel, and I was sad, shut down, and closed off—not exactly how a girl imagines she will feel after a proposal. And then, while he was sleeping, I got incredibly sick. I threw up and couldn't stop crying. Looking back, I realized that life was not going to let me move forward with this decision.

I knew what the right decision was, but my change demons were working overtime, filling me with insecurity. I was terrified of the situation I now found myself in. I struggled with the fear of making the wrong decision, fear of being alone afterward, fear of what others would say and think, and fear of never being proposed to again. I doubted my intuition, doubted my decision-making abilities, doubted if I would ever be happy again, and doubted that people would understand why I had turned down such a proposal.

About twenty-four hours later, I began to trust myself and found the faith and courage to say no to a life with this man. It was very, very difficult. But it was the beginning of being 100 percent true to myself. I could not disappear into this externally perfect relationship. Life had a different plan for me.

After turning down the proposal I felt massive liberation and freedom, but my change demons were far from gone. I was ashamed of how I would be judged and how I had let this happen. I felt guilty about hurting this man and guilty about not being honest and direct much earlier in our relationship. I blamed myself for not honoring my intuition, for not listening to the signs, for saying yes first and then having to say no. When I wasn't blaming myself, I blamed the man for not being the person I wanted him to be, for not understanding me better.

> *When your car tank is empty, you don't sit and get depressed and think it's permanent. You go fill it up. It's the same with life— when you're running on empty, go fill up your tank with a better thought, emotion or action and get on with life.*
> *—Esther Hicks*

And then I felt impatient. I was impatient with the grieving and healing process. I wanted life to show me the next man who was right for me ASAP.

Today, I know that although this twenty-four-hour engagement was painful, it was also incredibly powerful. It helped me find my faith and my trust while encouraging me to speak up for what I believed. I was able to forgive myself for ending up in such a predicament, to honor the event as a great lesson, and to wait very, very patiently for the right man to enter my life. And it also strengthened my change muscle—yet again!

Change Demon One: Fear

Fear is like a heat-seeking missile. You can't run away from it, hide from it, duck it. . . . But if you walk right at it, it misses you completely. It goes right past you, as if it were just an illusion.
—Richard Machowicz, television
host and former U.S. Navy SEAL

It's natural to be fearful of change. Whenever change happens, you are being asked to deal, yet again, with the uncertainty of a new future. Just when you get used to the way things are, change rears its head and throws you off balance. This is true even for those wonderful changes we have been dreaming about and hoping for all our lives, like finally getting married, having a child, or getting that new job or promotion.

Susan, for example, dreamed of having a baby for as long as she could remember. So when she found herself pregnant in her early thirties, she was surprised at her initial lack of joy. Instead of excitement and anticipation, she felt a serious sense of loss. She mourned her youth, which she thought was now officially over, and was filled with fear and doubt about her ability to be a good parent. Only after months of questioning and uncertainty did she begin to view the life that was growing inside of her as a gift. She realized that the baby was coming whether she was ready or not, so she decided to translate all of her doubt into trust, and in doing so she found a sense of faith that all would be OK. She even started to look forward to her baby's birth.

During change it's normal to experience many different types of fear:

- Fear of the future and of the unknown

- Fear of not being safe

- Fear of the reactions of loved ones

- Fear of no longer knowing who you are once something important in your identity has changed

- Fear of not being able to control other people and circumstances

- Fear of not being loved

- Fear of being alone

- Fear of not having enough money

- Fear of not being good enough

- Fear that your greatest dreams—getting married, having a baby—won't come true

When you take a deeper look at all of the things that you fear, notice that fear is an emotion that exists only in regard to the future. Worry and anxiety come from imagining terrible scenarios that could occur in the future instead of focusing on what is actually happening in the present moment. Focus on where you are right now; this will help to alleviate fears of what may happen down the line. By looking at your fears this way, you see that the probability of what you fear happening is much lower than your mind would have you believe. Rather than being scared, be curious as to what this change could possibly mean. Focus on the facts—what is true, what you know for sure—instead of imagining a gloomy future. The reality is that not a single person on the planet knows what is going to happen—not even in the next hour. So why waste time creating negative scenarios? The only thing you need to do right now is choose a better thought about this change and a better, brighter image of your future.

Get Familiar with Fear

Before this change, you likely held the illusion that you had control over your life. You probably thought, *I decide what happens, when, how, and with whom.* But undoubtedly, when going through the first thirty days of change—and beyond—we are reminded that we are not in control. This is often terrifying to consider. We miss the security we once had, even if it was an illusion.

> *One has really nothing in the world to fear. One becomes fearless when one understands the power of the soul.*
> —*Mahatma Gandhi*

But it's essential to move away from this attachment to safety and security and to start seeing the value in being slightly uncomfortable, to walking where there is no clearly defined path, to not knowing what might be around the corner.

Fear of change is often the excuse we use to justify not turning that corner and moving forward. But ask yourself, *Can I still live my life while the fear is present?* Yes, you can. Can something be born from this change, this fear, or even this loss? Yes, it can. Can you start focusing on the solutions instead of on the challenges you are facing? Yes, you can.

In our culture, we are much too focused on trying to get rid of fear and too little focused on learning to live with fear and incorporating it into our daily lives and actions. That's one of the secrets of people who take big risks and who make changes quickly: they have the same amount of fear as anyone else, but for them it's not an unfamiliar, threatening emotion. It's something they have encountered before. They are not paralyzed by it; in fact, they expect it. They know that fear will come, but they also know that they have made it through change and fear countless times before.

Take Angi. At the young age of twenty-four, she was diagnosed with stage-three breast cancer. She received treatment and went into remission. But at twenty-nine her cancer returned. This very courageous young woman had a total of seventeen surgeries and a double mastectomy. Now, at thirty-five, she is finally cancer free, but fear continues to be a part of her life. However, her primary fear today is not that the cancer will return. As a young woman who has undergone extensive reconstructive surgery, she worries more about having a "normal life," with friends, boyfriends, and hopefully even marriage and children.

But she doesn't allow herself to become paralyzed by the fear of how others will react to her physical changes; instead, she continues to live her life. She works, dates, and is like any other thirtysomething. "If somebody can't accept who I am and what I have gone through, I know that this person is not right for me," she says. "But it's still scary every time you have to explain a very personal side of your life. I think my biggest fear is more about people accepting me for me." Still, with every day, week, and month her fear seems to have less power over her. "Life took me down this path, and I have now found faith in myself, in how strong I have become."

Angi shows us that the only worthwhile reaction to change is to go along with it. Don't fight the reality that now exists in your life. Once we accept that we can't control the external events, people, and circumstances in our lives, we also see what we *can* control: our attitude, how we embrace change, and our reactions to change.

The Fear Antidote: Faith

> *My faith is brightest in the midst of impenetrable darkness.*
> —Mahatma Gandhi

When fear shows up, find your faith. Faith in what? When speaking of faith, I mean faith in oneself, or in something bigger than us. We need to have faith in our fellow human beings; faith in the values of love, compassion, and forgiveness; faith that things are always getting better. I also speak of faith in God, the Divine, the universe, or whatever spiritual belief or religion works for you.

But not all faith is created equal. In fact, there is a difference between blind faith and real faith. *Blind faith* is what often happens when we believe that God or someone else will fix everything. We think this change happened *to* us, not *for* or *because of*

> ### *Don't fear change, embrace it.*
> ### *—Anthony J. D'Angelo*

us, so we believe we're not responsible and that we don't need to do anything to make things better. For example, I know someone with cancer who regularly says, "If Jesus wants me to heal, he will heal me. He suffered, so I can, too. Other than that, I will keep on living my life as before. There is nothing I can do."

Real faith means you are a full and active participant in change. So yes, you can have cancer, pray about it, and give it up to God to help you heal; but you can also change some of your lifestyle habits, perhaps by locating the source of stress in your life that may have contributed to your illness, changing your diet, and exercising. Real faith means that you work hard, take as much action as you can, but surrender to *how* something happens and *when* something happens. This is the ultimate surrender—to have faith in the face of fear.

There is an ancient parable of a woman who is sick and goes to see a wise man. He tells her to boil stones in hot water so they are just hot enough to be swallowed. Then he tells her to eat the small stones twice a day while repeating a healing mantra. After a few weeks, the woman's signs of sickness disappear completely. It is a miracle. One day her son comes home from his travels and is overjoyed to see his mother in radiant health. He inquires as to what has healed her, and she excit-

> *Whether or not it is clear to you, no doubt the universe is unfolding as it should.*
> *—Max Ehrmann*

edly explains the methods the old man suggested. The son, somewhat of a healer himself, agrees with the stones treatment but tells her that the mantra she has been saying is the wrong one for her illness and that she should say something different. Within a week of following his suggestion, the mother's signs of sickness begin to return, and soon her body is once again riddled with disease.

What happened? Her faith had been destroyed by her son. Not that her son's intention was evil, but he inadvertently caused his mother to doubt and question her recovery, which made her fearful and unsure. She believed with every fiber of her being that she would get better, but once her faith was questioned, the outcome changed.

Don't let anyone throw your faith into doubt, especially when you are going through a change and fear is present. People will always find reasons for you not to trust, so that they can impose their beliefs and views on you. But nothing is more powerful than what you yourself choose to believe.

Place your burden at the feet of the Lord of the Universe who
accomplishes everything.
Remain all the time steadfast in the heart, in the
transcendental Absolute.
God knows the past, present and future.
He will determine the future for you and accomplish the work.
What is to be done will be done at the proper time. Don't worry.
Abide in the heart and surrender your acts to the divine.

—Ramana Maharshi,
Indian teacher and author

Nine Quick Ways to Make Fear Disappear

1. Don't be afraid of the unfamiliar.

This new transition and phase probably doesn't feel or look like
something from the past, so your automatic response and reaction is to be fearful. You say: *This is not familiar, it's new territory. I
don't know the way through.* But the fact that you're in a new place
doesn't mean that your life is ruined. Sometimes the change may
even open up a chapter in your life that you could never have
foreseen. Sometimes life really wants you to make huge leaps into
the unknown.

2. Acknowledge your fears, and remain realistic.

First, simply acknowledge that you feel afraid. Often it's not fear
that stops you, it's hiding the fear. Then identify what's triggering
this feeling. Perhaps it's fear of losing money or fear of losing your
standing in the professional world. Being gentle with your fears,
seeing them for what they are—illusions and events in the future

that were created by your mind—restores a sense of safety. Ask yourself about the likelihood of the following scenarios: How likely is it really that you will never be in another relationship? That you will never find work again? That you will never get pregnant? That your new job or promotion won't work out?

3. Act while experiencing fear.

Everyone feels fear; it's a natural part of doing something new. Although you can't do much to make the fear disappear, you can manage it. I used to have—and still sometimes have—a serious fear of speaking in public. Over the years, I turned down speaking engagements, speeches, and meetings for fear of not being able to speak in front of others. But as I have built my company, I am asked to speak on a weekly basis. Even today, before conferences and even some important meetings, I still feel anxiety on every level. I sweat and my heart races. The difference is that I have now learned to *manage my fear* by replacing it with thoughts of trust and faith—in my abilities and in life's guidance. I go through a little routine beforehand where I remind myself that things usually work out just fine and then I call upon my connection to my spirit to help and guide me. And I breathe deeply and start talking.

> *You fell down the first time you tried to walk. You almost drowned the first time you tried to swim. . . . Don't worry about failure. My suggestion to each of you: Worry about the chances you miss when you don't even try.*
> **—Orson Swett Marden**

4. Ask yourself if it's really fear.

Sometimes what we call fear is really just an unwillingness to move—procrastination or laziness that comes from low self-esteem. Are you using fear as an excuse not to act? Do any of the following statements ring true?

- I don't want to move because I don't want to start all over again.

- I don't want to leave my job because I don't want to take the time to research job leads, to interview, to possibly be rejected and then have to pick myself up again.

- I don't want to leave this abusive relationship because I don't want to be alone and have to find my way by myself.

- I can't stop drinking because I don't want to feel left out at a party when all my friends are drinking.

It's not always fear that holds people back. What could it be for you as you face this change now?

5. Realize that change is inevitable.

Change will happen even if you are paralyzed with fear. Today you may think, *I will never leave this relationship; I don't have the money or knowledge to take care of myself.* Sure, your fears may delay the change a few months or years, but that change *will* likely happen. My parents took more than ten years from when they first considered divorce to finally decide to do it. Both were full of fear. Did their fears disappear? No. Did they face them in the end by realizing that they had the ability to overcome any negative scenario they could imagine? Absolutely. It eventually became clear—as it does with every change if it is allowed to run its course—that the divorce was probably the best thing that could have happened and that my parents would be happier out of their marriage.

When is the right time to make a change? There is no magic formula for answering this question. Your simply asking it may mean that life has a new and better plan for you. For example, if you have been considering a career change for some time, the idea won't just fade away if you ignore it; eventually you will have to act. The same goes for a relationship change or any other change that has started to linger in your awareness.

6. Become an observer.

The next time change happens, take a moment to detach and observe how you are feeling. Say to yourself: *This is me, in this room, hearing this news and having these feelings. I am anxious. I am excited. I am nervous. I am scared. I am sad. I am confused.* Whatever you feel is fine.

My friend Jen was engaged to the man she thought was her soul mate. They moved in together and began to plan for their summer wedding. But then the unthinkable happened. They were in a restaurant while on vacation, and out of the blue her fiancé said, "I don't want to be married. I don't want to be with you." And that was it.

Jen describes the moment as a sort of out-of-body, detached experience, where she became an actor in this absurd theatrical play. Here she was, in a charming restaurant in a beautiful place, facing a man she loved. And he was telling her she was now single. She could feel the emotions in her body very clearly.

What Jen had unknowingly done was protect herself from the drama of the moment, the emotions, and the crisis. She was able to find her thinker and observer, the part of her that could handle this, and just *be* with the situation that was happening. Instead of reacting or overreacting, she remained calm, her mind clear, in the face of terrible news. The purpose of distancing herself was not to go into a state of denial. Of course, Jen grieved this loss. But stepping back allowed her to recognize that a big part of her was safe, certain, and in control.

> *Listen to your fear with a wise ear. Your goal is not to rid yourself of fear, but to recognize its presence and to view it as a less powerful force than the wisdom and faith that reside inside of you. We fear because we have forgotten how strong we are.*

Fear can be sitting next to you in the passenger seat, but you are still driving the car.

7. Ask yourself if this is really your fear.

You may discover that some of the fears you're carrying aren't your own. Identify what the fear is, and then ask yourself what is really behind it. Is it your mother's fear, your dad's, your partner's, your friend's? For example, plenty of women I have met are scared that they will never get married, but when they look inside they find that they've taken on their parents' fear of never having grandkids. Plenty of men worry that they won't find a job that pays them enough money, but when they look inside they find that they've taken on society's notion that a man won't be able to take care of a family unless he has a certain income.

8. Get back in the flow.

Replace the fear with habits that are comfortable for you, with actions that produce hope, and with anything that encourages you to physically move! Moving actually dissipates negative fearful energy within the body. Start doing the things that give you certainty—little things, familiar things, and routines you have always done. Yes, something big may have changed in your life, but lots of stuff hasn't. So ground yourself in things that make you feel safe, that still are—and always will be—there. Go to the mall, the movies, or church. Visit friends, take a walk, or hit the gym. Or eat at a favorite restaurant, go home to see a parent, or give support to someone else in need.

9. See yourself one year—or five years—from today.

Focus on the positive picture you have of your future. What are you doing differently? What kind of thoughts are you thinking? What actions are you taking? Keep picturing yourself living happily in the future, and in a matter of time the fear you feel today will have dissipated as you see how life is unfolding.

✔ Take Action

1. Identify moments during changes in your life, when you felt fear. How did you conquer the fear? Now, recognize how you felt once you moved past it.

2. What are you doing today that you used to fear?

Change Demon Two: Doubt

Our doubts are traitors, and make us lose the good we oft might win by fearing to attempt.

—William Shakespeare,
Measure for Measure

Most of the time we're pretty sure of ourselves. We know where we work, who loves us, how much money we have, where we live, who our friends are, how we look, the status of our health, and so on. That's why change makes us so uncomfortable. Suddenly we are no longer in the driver's seat. If we are handed a change, we want to know immediately what it means. And if we initiate a change, we want to know that we will succeed. We long to see what the future might bring. During this time, it's likely we will become pessimistic: we doubt that good things will come our way, and we doubt that we will pull through. If it's a decision we made, we doubt that it was the right one. And if it's a change we're initiating, we doubt that we will succeed in a reasonable amount of time.

When life has changed, we also often doubt that anything like a God exists. Instead, we turn to beliefs like *If there was a God, he would never have allowed this to happen.* When we are in the midst of a change, it's futile to look for whether God played a role or didn't. Eventually, we have to come back to things we can control—our own optimism and hope, our own feelings and actions.

They say, "Good things come in threes," but for my friend Toby, doubt came in threes as well. He had to endure the divorce of his parents, the financial challenges of starting up a business, and a breakup with his long-term girlfriend, all at once. And all of these changes quickly led him to great doubt. He doubted himself as a man, as a CEO, as a son, as a friend, and as someone who had anything to give back to the world. Then, eventually, he began to see that he did not have an ounce of control over what life was throwing at him, that he needed to surrender to that fact and trust that he would come through it all. Today, Toby is in a new relationship and has made positive changes in his professional life. He is healthy and happy and knows not to doubt where life is leading him.

The Doubt Antidote: Surrender

When we are faced with change, surrendering is often what we need to do the most; it is a key step in building courage and eliminating doubt. When doubt shows up, let go a little, get in touch with your intuition a bit more, and trust that things will work themselves out and become clear. Tremendous strength and relief come with giving up control of how life may go and accepting the reality of your situation.

Imagine yourself in a boxing ring with your opponent: life. There you are, fighting, sweating, and believing you can win. But it's completely impossible to beat life. Still we fight, because we think we can come out on top and beat life at its own game—even though life made up all the rules, can change them at any time, and has infinite power and wisdom. Life can knock us out or give us victory in the blink of an eye. Seems futile, no?

I was talking with some guy friends of mine who all agreed to throw in the towel, surrender, and stop doubting and fighting life. One was forty and single; he had expected to be married by now. Another, a few years younger, never imagined he would still be in the same job. The last guy was a widow, a thirty-four-year-old single father who wanted to remarry. They all realized there was no point in trying to control their lives. And they found this realization incredibly freeing. They still had desires and dreams, but they had surrendered the *how* and the *when* something would happen, and in doing so they helped to put themselves on the path toward the next positive phase of life.

> *It's ok to have doubts,*
> *just don't feed and*
> *entertain them.*
> *— Bernie Siegel*

Doubt also shows up because we spend too much time asking other people for their advice and opinions. These external influences can take us further away from finding the clarity and certainty we are looking for. Trust yourself more; don't turn to other people until you've consulted your own sense of direction and guidance. You have a lot of inner wisdom.

We need to remember that we can continue to trust despite feelings of confusion, chaos, and doubt. Believe it or not, these opposing emotions can exist at the same time. The first thirty days are a time when we must surrender to what is coming our way and remember that things will get better and that there is a good reason this change is happening. Just as a plane in turbulence stabilizes itself when the pilot lets go of the controls, so is it with our lives. We will go through stormy patches, and we will be asked to trust, to let go, and to wait and see what's on the other side.

Change Demon Three: Impatience

> *Never think that God's delays are God's denials. Hold on; hold fast; hold out. Patience is genius.*
> —Comte de Buffon

Frank learned of the power of patience when he left his job at a Wall Street firm to create an environmentally friendly hedge fund.

Making the transition took over a year's work and tested him on many levels, especially his commitment to his vision. Frank soon understood that when making changes it's essential to be patient and let the universe do its work. "Making big shifts can take time and will happen when the universe is convinced you are ready for the change and not before," he says. "The more I did the work and let go of the expectations of the outcome, the more things flowed." Instead of wasting energy telling himself that he was getting nowhere in pursuit of his dream, he decided that he had done all the work he could do, and so he openly said to the universe, "I let go of all my expectations and hand over the outcome and timing to you." This change in mind-set brought quick results: Frank thought he was going to get an offer from one firm, and within a week he received two important calls that set his new career in motion with an even better company.

It's natural to want to speed up change. Change brings something new and different to our lives and can leave us disoriented, unsure, and stressed. We want to go back to living our lives the way they were before. We want certainty again. But we can't accelerate change. We have absolutely no control over the tempo of life. This is the difference between the pace of the universe and the

> *Do you have the patience*
> *to wait till your mud settles*
> *and the water is clear?*
> *Can you remain unmoving*
> *till the right action arises*
> *by itself?*
> **—Tao Te Ching**

pace of the mind. The universe works on its own schedule even as the mind has already decided that the change process is taking too long and tries, in vain, to speed it up. We are constantly in search of a fast fix for our feelings and emotions. If something hurts—and change often hurts—we long for it to be over ASAP. But sometimes the best thing to do is to just sit and be with what we're feeling.

The next time you find yourself trying to breeze through a change, be still and let the process unfold and develop in the way it needs to. Be very patient with yourself when going through transitions; don't let your emotions or negative beliefs and assumptions get the better of you. You will find that hopelessness, despair, and sadness run their course and that one day they just go away. You don't know when that will happen—it's not for you to decide—but it always does. Think of the many times you were incredibly anxious or worried. Do you remember exactly when those feelings ended? Not really. So just be patient; this period will transform. And remember that something is being revealed to you during change, so look for it.

Many times, we will go through a change and have the false impression that we have made no progress and that things are taking forever to turn around. Remember the old saying "Well begun is half done." You cannot see the steps you have already taken in the right direction. Keep choosing better thoughts and emotions, and as long as you remain patient with the natural unfolding of what is happening and what is coming, your life will rearrange itself faster than you thought.

The Impatience Antidote: Endurance

Every change depends largely on your endurance, or the ability to wait for the new phase of your life to progress. Change—whether physical, mental, or emotional—takes time. Once you accept this simple fact, you will be able to better confront your own expectations about how fast change should happen and deal with the transition in successive and realistic stages. When you replace impatience with endurance—the part of you that can absolutely keep going and be patient even when the rest of you wants to give up—you are demonstrating supreme strength and grace. All heroes, athletes, and successful businesspeople will attest that change often takes longer than they'd planned or imagined. Endurance is about putting in the work during change: there are new decisions to make, new actions to take, and a new mind-set to embrace.

People often don't understand the meaning of patience. Too many of us believe it means sitting back and doing nothing. But patience is actually the science of being at peace. This doesn't mean nonaction. If you are looking for a job, for

> *Be patient toward all that is unsolved in your heart and try to love the questions themselves, like locked rooms and like books that are written in a very foreign tongue. Do not now seek the answers, which cannot be given to you because you would not be able to live them. And the point is, to live everything. Live the questions now. Perhaps you will find them gradually, without noticing it, and live along some distant day into the answer.*
> *—Rainer Maria Rilke*

example, you still need to scan job postings and send out résumés. If you want to heal a damaged relationship, you need to talk things through or seek out professional help. Too many people hide behind being "patient," and as they wait, doing nothing, the change begins to feel heavy and impossible to move past. So get going and do what you can, knowing that you are being assisted by life and that the mystery of the next phase of life will be revealed in time.

Change Demon Four: Blame

The search for someone to blame is always successful.
—Robert Half

Leo experienced the power of blame after over ten years as a successful soccer player. "Two minutes before the end of a big game, I scored the winning goal," he recalls. "As I kicked the ball into the net, the goalie—who at six-three and two-hundred-forty pounds was considerably bigger than me—charged toward me at a full sprint. He slid into my legs, and the force of impact was so great that it shattered the bones beneath my knees into six individual pieces." The damage was so severe that Leo's doctors suggested amputating one of his legs.

Leo spent weeks in intense pain and recovery, blaming the goalie for much of his discomfort. *How could he have done this to me?* he asked himself daily.

But eventually Leo shifted his perspective on the accident—and on this change: "What I didn't know at the time, but I've since learned, is events like these are meaningless except for the meaning that we bring to them. Many people may think that my injury was a tragedy, but it actually turned out to be a blessing—the beginning of a new journey."

Though the goalie never apologized for the incident or ever spoke to him after that night, Leo not only stopped blaming him, but also found it within himself to forgive him: "If given the chance, I would hug this man and thank him for unknowingly giving me the most amazing gift. I think about what my life would have been like if this had never happened to me."

The injury inspired Leo to tap into a deep reserve of strength and faith as he fought against the amputation suggested by his medical team; he now has full use of both of his legs. And after a lifetime of focusing solely on soccer, he has expanded his athletic interests to including competing in Ironman® triathlons. Most important, his process of healing required him to slow down, which enabled him to start a family. Today, Leo speaks nationally on the power of taking responsibility for your own change, learning to forgive, and never getting stuck in a cycle of blame.

In the first thirty days of any change, we all look for someone to blame for the pain or stress that we're experiencing. I've met people who have blamed their dog for their not being able to change careers, or their parents, who died years ago, for their failed relationships.

But this blame game is really an expression of anger, disappointment, and, most often, hurt. We believe we *have* to blame someone or something because we feel so let down. We blame instead of expressing our true emotions, because the latter makes us vulnerable.

Blame—or anger if that's how it's showing up for you—keeps us from taking responsibility and from accepting the reality of what is happening in our lives. And when we blame something or someone for the change that has come into our world, it keeps us from having to do the inner work of healing or the outer work of having to take action. It helps us avoid our feelings, procrastinate, and delay important decisions related to the change.

Blame also gives us a false sense of control by making it seem as if we know why something has happened. When we blame, at least it *feels* like we are right and others are wrong. But blame won't ever change what has happened. You can blame a highly ambitious colleague for your recent loss of a job or your husband for your child's misbehavior, but blame gives you nothing. It actually delays the speed at which you move through change. Instead of blaming, ask yourself what it is that *you* can be doing now in response to what has changed.

✓ Take Action

Take the twenty-four-hour no-blame challenge. This is how it works: pick a day, look at the time, and for the next twenty-four hours do not blame anything or anyone for what happens in your life. That includes problems you encounter with traffic, weather, work, friends, family, and even God. Be extra cautious not to blame yourself, either. If you find that a day is easy for you, try a week. You'll soon see a pattern that will reveal who gets most of your blame energy. Is it you? Your spouse? Your child? Your job? The city you live in?

Blame is what we do to distract ourselves from what has happened, what has changed, what our reality is now. When we blame, we always turn to the past, looking back and wondering how things *could* have ended up. Moreover, blame depends on assumptions. We assume that if someone else had acted in a different way, none of this would have happened to us—even though there's no guarantee of that. What is in the past is over and done, and replaying the scenario over and over in your mind won't lead you anywhere productive.

The most destructive thing we do is blame ourselves. When a relationship breaks up, for example, our first instinct is to wonder what *we* did wrong, what *we* could have said differently, and how it was *our* fault. We blame ourselves when we are laid off. We blame ourselves when we can't get pregnant or when we have a miscarriage. We blame ourselves when no one seems to want to be in a relationship with us. We blame ourselves if our kids get sick. We blame ourselves for not having the courage to change jobs or finally lose weight.

What we don't see are the myriad reasons beyond ourselves that may have caused these life changes. Perhaps your breakup had nothing to do with you and everything to do with the fact that you and your partner weren't compatible. Or perhaps you were laid off for economic reasons that had nothing to do with your own performance. Or perhaps life has a different plan and there are, for now, invisible reasons something happened.

> *[Blame] is a very common, ancient, well-perfected device for trying to feel better. Blame others. Blaming is a way to protect your heart, trying to protect what is soft and open and tender in yourself. Rather than own that pain, we scramble to find some comfortable ground.*
> *—Pema Chödrön*

By blaming yourself, you become stuck in old patterns, old emotions, and old ways of looking at life. Blame distracts you from looking at the facts, free from emotion. And so it keeps you from doing what needs to be done—making changes in how you look after your health, learning to handle your finances, packing up and moving, or forgiving someone. Stop telling yourself, *I should have done this* or *I should never have said that.* What's the point? Blame has never helped anyone achieve anything.

The real question, then, is *What can I do now?* Once blame isn't an option, what is your alternative?

The Blame Antidote: Honesty

Start by giving up your excuses.

Everyone has a story or a list of excuses for why change has occurred. But the best antidote to blame is honesty, not excuses. When we are honest, we accept the reality of our current situation and face up to the work that needs to be done to move through it, regardless of who else might have been involved. Honesty doesn't allow us to sit with our excuses and become lazy. It inspires us to transform our situation and to raise our standards about the kind of life we want to live.

> *God, grant me the serenity*
> *To accept the things I*
> *cannot change;*
> *Courage to change the*
> *things I can;*
> *And wisdom to know the*
> *difference.*
> *—The Serenity Prayer*

Women often blame their husbands for the breakup of their marriages. I once met a woman named Joanne. Twelve years after her divorce, she still believed that her ex-husband was the only person responsible for their breakup. She was stuck on that belief, and as a result, nothing in her life had progressed. Sure, she wasn't wearing a wedding ring anymore, but other than that, her inner and outer worlds hadn't really changed.

Nothing great has ever been created out of blame. Nothing. All blame does is immobilize you and give you an excuse not to learn and move on with the rest of your life.

Sometimes when you put a mirror up to people's lives, there is a moment of clarity. Joanne saw something she hadn't wanted to see before. During her marriage, she had focused only on the kids. She had given up her dreams and paid no attention to being a loving wife, and because she stopped focusing on herself, she also put on an enormous amount of weight. Eventually she realized that she, too, shared responsibility for the divorce. This didn't excuse her ex-husband's behavior, but now she could see things from his perspective.

Today, Joanne is truly a happier person. She is no longer burdened by blame. She is now a shining example for her children, who feel relieved that their mother has moved beyond saying bad things about their father.

☑Take Action

Take a minute to write down all the stories and excuses you keep telling yourself to explain a change, and then ask yourself, *Is this really true?* For example:

- He (or she) broke up with me because . . .
- I am sick because . . .
- I went bankrupt because . . .
- I am getting divorced because . . .
- I am single because . . .
- I can't lose weight because . . .
- My boss hates me because . . .
- My stepmother doesn't like me because . . .
- I can't get a job because . . .
- I don't speak to my father because . . .

Don't look to place blame, but rather explore how your behavior honestly helped to create the problem or worsen it. After all, the person you blame has often moved on to bigger and better things. You deserve such things, too. Can you recognize your pattern of blame? Choosing to forgive someone (including yourself) is often the catalyst for major change.

Let go of labels.

Don't judge change as being either good or bad. Just let it happen.
One and the same thing can at the same time be good, bad, and
indifferent, e.g., music is good to the melancholy, bad to those
who mourn, and neither good nor bad to the deaf.

—Baruch Spinoza,
Dutch philosopher

Most people would say getting married is a beautiful thing and
divorce is a terrible thing. But ask them a few years later and you
might get a very different answer. Others would say having a
child was the best thing that ever happened to them; but when
the child is grown and doesn't talk to them anymore, they sing a
different tune. Have you ever lost a job and been devastated only
to find, after the initial shock, that it was a blessing in disguise?
Or been dumped only to think, after a few months in the arms of
your new beloved, *Thank goodness that person let me go*?

Wingate Paine, author of *The Book of Surrender (A Journey to
Self-Awareness Inspired by the Words of Emmanuel),* once wrote:
"Bad is how we see those experiences whose part in our growth
we do not yet understand." Stay open to change, observe your
life, step back—and *wonder.* There are always multiple realities,
multiple possibilities, for what something may mean and what a
change might lead to.

The Zen masters taught that one should never resent a difficult
event or change but should await an understanding of its full purpose. As one story goes:

A farmer who had just bought a stallion came to find a Zen
master after it fled the stable. He said to him: "Master! The
horse ran away! The horse ran away!"

The Zen master said to the farmer, "Who knows if this is a good thing or bad thing?"

Three days later, the same farmer came before the Zen master, this time in tears. He said that his only son, his only help at the farm, had been thrown from one of the horses and had broken his back. He was therefore in a cast, and could no longer work.

The Zen master repeated: "Who knows if this is a good thing or bad thing?"

Several days later, a group of soldiers came to the farm. They were recruiting young men of the region to go to war. As the farmer's son was in a cast, they didn't enlist him. All the other sons in the village were taken that day to go and fight.

Change Demon Five: Guilt

Guilt is anger directed at ourselves.
—Peter McWilliams

We all know what it's like to feel guilty. Guilt can start in the present moment, based on something recent that has happened, or it may have begun many years back. People can feel guilty about anything: what kind of a parent they are, the way they work, their weight, what they eat, what they said to someone, the money they spent, a decision they made. The list is endless. What we need to remember is that feeling guilt and regret is a natural process of growing. The guilt is there to wake us up, to help us recognize our humanness. Start to view guilt as part of your emotional guidance system, as one more emotion that is letting you know you are slightly off course. The quicker you let go of guilt, the quicker you will move through the change.

The Guilt Antidote: Forgiveness

When you are feeling guilty, the real stumbling block is an inability to forgive yourself. You don't always have the answers. Sometimes you mess up. Sometimes you say the wrong thing. Sometimes you will do anything to change what has happened. And sometimes you will make the same mistake over and over. But if you make the effort to forgive yourself, guilt will be a thing of the past.

One of my best friends got divorced after ten years of marriage and two kids. He has still not found a way to forgive himself for this decision. When you look into his eyes, you see his guilt. In his mind, he should have done things differently. He feels guilty about what the divorce may mean for his kids and for everyone else who was involved.

> *Guilt is perhaps the most painful companion of death!*
> *— Coco Chanel*

Even though the split happened three years ago, he is still in a prison of guilt and doesn't realize the door is open and he has the power to escape. Whenever he tries to let go of the guilt, he stumbles upon something else to feel guilty about. He thinks of his ex-wife, or his parents, or something his kids may have said. He is a sponge for guilt, soaking it up everywhere he goes.

What he most needs is to walk out of his prison cell by fully forgiving himself for the past. He needs to take his power back from what his guilty conscience has been feeding him. But until he says, "Enough. I am full. I have eaten enough guilt," there will always be more guilt to consume. You need to push the plate of guilt away, saying, "No more. This isn't good for me." It's time to go on a no-guilt diet.

The change demons are there to serve us. They all have a unique role. They all help refine our actions and outlook. Guilt can be a huge blessing when we use it well, when it sparks a change in our behavior, when we finally take a stand for something or someone, when we finally not only forgive ourselves but also ask for forgiveness from someone we may have hurt. Guilt is not always a bad thing; it can be a way out of a pattern of behavior if we choose to see it that way.

☑ Take Action

What do you feel guilty about? It may be something to do with your parents, your relationship, your work, your weight, or a lie you told.

How much longer do you want to live with this guilt?

What is the truth about each of these situations? How would someone else see it? How would God see it?

For each of the things you identified, ask yourself whether you can forgive yourself and replace the guilt with a better emotion. How can you make the situation even slightly better today?

Change Demon Six: Shame

Once we realize that imperfect understanding is the human condition there is no shame in being wrong, only in failing to correct our mistakes.

—George Soros

When we are in the middle of a change, we tend to believe everything our mind tells us. If our mind tells us that we are stupid, that we are unloved, that we aren't good enough, that we are alone, and that we won't succeed at changing, we will usually believe it and hide from the rest of the world, ashamed.

Shame is often present when you do something that is not easily accepted by society or your tribe. The people who surround you often have many ideas of how your life is supposed to unfold and are usually not hesitant to express them to you. This is an absurd amount of pressure and weight for you to carry on your shoulders. Living up to people's expectations is an incredibly heavy burden that none of us need to bear.

When a change happens or you find the courage to change something, shame tends to show up. This requires taking yet another stand and finding even more courage to face people's perception of your actions. We are all ashamed of things that did or didn't happen to us. You may have been diagnosed with cancer, discovered that your child is an addict, or been fired. Perhaps you're in debt, don't own your own home, didn't go to college, or have been trying to lose weight for years. The quicker we unhook from the perceptions of others, the quicker positive, healing energy will flow through us. Don't let the tribe dictate every aspect of your life: what you do, what you wear, whom you marry, if you divorce or move to a new city. Shame also comes from having to ask for help, having to start something new, having to admit to people that we don't know everything, or having to be not as together as others may think we are or should be. We all so desperately want to look good.

When shame comes up, use it as an opportunity to test your strength, to take your power back, and to move forward with your actions and choices despite others' perceptions and expectations. Be a pioneer. Do the unexpected. Cut the umbilical cord still tying you to society and your tribe.

The Shame Antidote: Honor

I remember being asked to speak at a conference in New York City about ten years ago. I was having a bad day, and I didn't want to go, but I had committed to the event, so I went. When I was asked to introduce myself, I literally froze. My breathing became tight and strained; my throat went dry; my face turned red. I could barely get three words out. I was horrified and disappointed in myself. But what I was really feeling was a massive amount of shame. I was ashamed that I would be perceived as a ridiculous fool instead of a successful, confident businesswoman. I was sure that I would be laughed at. I had wanted to look good, sound good, be admired and respected. But life gave me a different outcome. All I wanted to do was hide and never speak again in public. It took me years to build up the confidence to stand in front of an audience again.

Eventually I accepted and honored my traumatic public-speaking experience. Honor comes from embracing all that has happened to you—the good and the bad; your choices, decisions, and mistakes. I looked back on that moment and asked it to reveal its lesson. I tried to understand why it had occurred. I soon realized that I was more concerned with looking good and being liked than with delivering anything of value to my audience. And when I talked about the experience with friends, they were shocked. They all thought I loved public speaking. But by sharing my anxieties openly and bringing them to light, I found that the situation wasn't as dire as I had imagined. I still had friends who loved and respected me, and I would be given many more chances to speak in public.

You learn so much more from your mistakes than your victories. I have since gone on to take incredible speaking, acting, and improv classes and have accepted that when I speak publicly, it's not about me. It's about what I'm giving the audience—how I can help.

There is a great story of a Cherokee grandfather talking to his grandson. The grandfather explains, "There are two wolves that live within each of us. One is filled with anger, hate, lust, blame, envy, fear, jealousy, and outrage at the injustices done to him. The other is filled with compassion, faith, kindness, humility, and understanding." The grandson asked him, "Grandfather, which wolf is stronger?" and the grandfather answered: "The one we feed."

As we go through each day, let's ask ourselves: "Which inner wolf am I feeding . . . the destructive wolf or the loving wolf?" If we realize that it is the destructive wolf we are feeding (with change demons), we owe it to ourselves and the world to do everything we can to make the loving wolf get stronger and more dominant.

Owning the change will set you free. The sooner you do this, the sooner you will feel a sense of relief.

Learning from Your Change Demons

We have 50–60,000 thoughts a day. 90% of them are negative.
—Deepak Chopra

In order to create a new, optimistic mind-set that will help you navigate change, it's essential to regain control over your negative thoughts and emotions. Make friends with all of your change demons. And become an expert at identifying which one is present. It's very liberating to meet them and to face them head-on. As you move through change you can begin to recognize them as they come up: *Ah, here is blame, there's guilt, now I'm feeling impatient,* and so on. Be with them; don't run from them. Shine a light on them; don't ignore them. If a demon shows up, acknowledge what it has to say and then gently replace it by choosing an emotion that will help you feel a little bit better.

You will start to see whether you are someone who blames everyone for everything or whether you tend to feel alone and ashamed. Or maybe you always feel guilty. Once you have identified your change demons and become friends with them (at least *friendly* with them), you can choose to flip the coin and replace them with something like surrender, honesty, or forgiveness.

When one of the change demons comes up, stop for a moment—as if you were in a car, heading in the wrong direction—and remember the change GPS. Ask yourself where you are now in terms of your feelings and emotions, and where you want to be. Focus on getting yourself to a place of feeling better, and you'll see just how quickly you move through change and begin pointing yourself in the direction of the next phase of your life.

The First 30 Days: What to Remember

1. There are six main change demons: fear, doubt, impatience, blame, guilt, and shame. As a part of the change GPS, they exist to guide you back on course. So even though they may feel painful, they are there to serve you. Recognize which demons are making this change harder for you.

2. Allow yourself to be human. We all feel these emotions. Be kinder and gentler toward yourself when your demons appear.

3. Every change demon can be replaced by a positive emotion and feeling, one that can help you move away from pain and suffering. You always have a choice to feel better. Be pickier about the emotions you hang out with! Here are the demons and their respective antidotes:

Demon	Antidote
1. Fear	Faith
2. Doubt	Surrender
3. Impatience	Endurance
4. Blame	Honesty
5. Guilt	Forgiveness
6. Shame	Honor

As you go the way of life, you will come to a great chasm. Jump. It is not as far as you think.
—Native American saying

5

The Gift of Acceptance

Resisting Change Is Not the Answer

Principle 5: People who successfully navigate change know that the quicker they accept the change, the less pain and hardship they will feel.

Let go of the idea of how life should be.

As we discussed in chapter 1, the beliefs you have about change can dramatically affect how you feel when going through it. But it's equally important to learn to accept the change that has come into your life. When you accept change, it means that you take in your new circumstances without fighting, arguing, explaining, or asking *What if?* Whenever I hear of someone who is having trouble accepting change, I always turn to an analogy I once heard (from *Teachings of Abraham* by Esther and Jerry Hicks)—of the boat in the river: when you resist change, it's as if you are rowing upstream against the current. Everything that is right for you now is ahead of you, so change becomes hard when you try to get back upstream to where you once were. When change happens, we often longingly look back to what we used to have or what we used to be. We don't like where the river (life) seems to be taking us, so we make major efforts to stop our movement. We cling to the rocks, we row vigorously back upstream, and that's what makes change tough!

But the reality is that whether we realize it or not, all we truly want is downstream now. And it's impossible to go back upstream anyway, so we have no choice but to let go of the oars and stop resisting. Soon our boat will naturally point itself in the right direction—it happens quite quickly once we stop fighting the current—and things will be less traumatic. During change, always remember: if you are in pain or stressed, it means you are rowing upstream. No matter how hard it may seem, settle in to what has happened, and move in the direction of the river. It knows where to take you.

When we don't accept change, we resist the forward momentum taking us to the next phase of our lives and remain stuck in what once was. It's easy to understand this concept, but it's much harder to make it happen in real life. Trust me, I know.

I spent the greater part of my adult life resisting the ways things were, wishing and hoping they would be something else. Only recently have I settled into the facts of my life, and in doing so I have discovered a sense of peace and contentment. Growing up all around the world, I felt my life to be a constant exercise in accepting things that were out of my control. I constantly had to adapt to new schools, friends, and cultures. But one of my biggest acceptance moments had nothing do with moving; it had to do with swimming. I grew up primarily in Hong Kong and started swimming when I was quite young. I quickly made the national swim team and was soon competing at meets around Asia. I swam four hours a day, from five to seven in the morning and from six to eight in the evening. I would go to bed with my swimsuit on to sneak in a few extra moments of sleep in the morning. Swimming was my passion. My coach told me that I'd make the Olympics. And I was on that path: I won medals, was one of the top female swimmers for the one-hundred-meter butterfly in Asia, and qualified for many of the pre-Olympic events.

Then my life abruptly changed. My dad decided that swimming was not a viable career option for me and that I should focus instead on my education, and he sent me to a strict girls' boarding school in England. So while a core unit of my swim team went on to the 1988 Olympics in Seoul, I found myself adjusting to a new school thousands of miles away from my family and friends. I went from training four hours a day to not training at all. I went from being a renowned swimmer to disappearing into the English countryside. I was

> **When you argue with reality, you lose, but only 100% of the time.**
> **—Byron Katie**

lonely and afraid. Swimming was all I had known. I spent many days feeling angry and hating my new environment, but there was nothing I could do. I had to accept the situation I was now in. With no other choice, I shifted my perspective, focused on my studies, and tried to get out as soon as possible. I graduated when I was sixteen. Life obviously had other plans for me.

The Optimist's Mind-Set: Accept Your Way Through Change

Every thought that begins with *I can't, I won't,* or *I don't* equals resistance. We can deny change or ignore change, but it is too powerful and impossible to resist for very long. Think of the ocean: no matter how ingenious an engineer you are, you can't stop the waves from crashing to shore. It's silly to think you are smarter than the waves or the natural direction in which things flow. The same goes for change. We can continually resist what's changed, but with time we eventually adjust to the new way of living. Think about it: After a painful divorce, both parties recover and meet other people. After losing your job, you find a better position. After being diagnosed with diabetes, you change your eating habits and soon feel better. And even after one of the most painful changes—the death of a loved one—you eventually find yourself adjusting to a new way of life.

Charlotte's older brother was killed in a bad accident, and it took her mother eleven years to finally accept the tragedy. She kept her son's room exactly the same as it was the day he died. For those eleven years she would go into his room and cry. "It cut my mom off for years of her life," Charlotte told me. "She didn't face reality, couldn't accept that she wasn't in control of this situation, and she couldn't see that people like me and her other friends needed her to come back to being with us." Finally, after grieving the tremendous loss, her mother came to see that she needed to accept the situation and did her best to move on with her life. She wrote a cookbook with all her favorite recipes, sold the house she had raised her children in, and gave her son's clothes away to a local homeless shelter.

We may have a step-by-step plan for how our lives are supposed to unfold, but as all of us have seen, life has its own plans; it's an illusion that we are in control. Accepting change is the best thing we can do for ourselves, because change happens whether we like it or not. It is absolutely unstoppable. Just look at the human body: we are born, we age and get wrinkles, and one day we will die. These are some of the most basic things in life that are out of our control; they can't be avoided. And if we can accept that some days will be warm and others cool, that some days we will be happy and others moody, we must learn to have the same acceptance of the other changes that affect our lives.

But learning to accept change doesn't mean you can't grieve your changes—even the positive ones. It's OK to be in the darkness for a little while. We'll talk about this more later, but remember that this is an important phase of going through change. Give yourself the space to feel sad, angry, frustrated, or afraid. You can cry, scream, throw things, and be generally ticked off at life. But when you've let it all out, begin to prepare yourself to move into the light. You do this by accepting what has happened.

Accepting the facts of the situation not only helps you transition from the past into the present, but also gives you a much clearer sense of what has actu-

> *Hence, there is a time to go ahead and a time to stay behind.*
> *There is a time to breathe easy and a time to breathe hard.*
> *There is a time to be vigorous and a time to be gentle.*
> *There is a time to gather and a time to release.*
> *Can you see things as they are And let them be all on their own?*
> *—Lao-tzu*

ally changed versus what hasn't changed. When we go through change it's easy to create a laundry list of all of the other "terrible" things that have happened to us. Sure, you may have recently ended a relationship, but you still have your family, friends, job, skills, passions, and creativity. Your best friend may have moved to another country, but you can still write and call, and you still have many other people in your life, lots of hobbies, and a job you enjoy. You have accepted change when you understand that right now you and your husband may be separated but that the rest of your life is still functioning; you still have a home and a child and a career. Make sure that you focus on all of the parts of your life that haven't changed. Those are the places that will give you the strength to move forward. Remember: Things just are—and the faster you accept this and take the right action, the freer you will be.

Reality Versus Illusion

When accepting a change, it's essential to acknowledge that something has indeed happened without making the new situation a fixed and permanent part of your life. This is a delicate balance, but as you readily accept more and more of the changes in your life, you will learn to differentiate reality from illusion. *Reality* is the absolute facts that make up your situation, that surround your change. *Illusion* is the idea we create around change, what we assume it means. Here is the difference: reality says your relationship has ended while illusion says you'll never meet anyone else, and you will never be happy again.

The sooner you accept that something has happened or needs to happen, the sooner you will move through the painful part of change and onto the next stage of life. You may be hesitant to accept a change because you feel that you are giving victory to it if you acknowledge it as truth. But when you accept your new circumstances, you are the one who is victorious, because the change doesn't have power over you anymore. If you resist the fact that you are overweight by keeping up the same poor eating and exercise habits, you will stay stuck in the same pattern of weight gain. But if you accept the reality and truth about your weight, you will be more motivated to change. When it comes to change, the truth really shall set you free.

A wonderful woman I know has always struggled with money. She has dreamed of becoming an actress for years, and she has courageously held firm to that path. The reality, however, is that she is broke. There are days when she can't afford to eat and days when she hates herself and feels like her whole life is falling apart. She believes that if she were to get a simple job that paid the bills, she would be selling out and would no longer be free to pursue her art. But again, reality states that she has no money and is in debt. She could have easily gotten a job, but she was so stuck in her illusion that she believed a day job would interfere with her ability to audition, that people wouldn't respect her as much for doing something else, and that no other job would be as exciting or interesting as acting. Eventually reality caught up with her. "I finally accepted that I was living under illusion. The reality is that a job would just help me pay some bills; it wouldn't be a reflection of who I was as a person. I pushed my pride out of the way and did what I needed to do," she says. By accepting reality she also increased her trust in where life was taking her. And as life would have it, while working at a restaurant she met the producer of major television show and in another she met the casting director of a big Hollywood movie in which she played a small part. Her advice: "Accept what is, face the facts, be honest with yourself, and then do what needs to be done."

Our Change Demons and Acceptance

Before you can accept the changes in your life, you have to recognize what triggers your resistance. As we learned in chapter 4, we most often resist change when one or more of our change demons appear. It is absolutely natural to experience fear, blame, impatience, guilt, doubt, or shame during change, but it's equally important to move past those feelings and onto one of understanding and acceptance.

Experiencing shame during change can make it very difficult to accept your new reality, because you are too busy worrying about the opinions you believe other people have formed about you. If you didn't get into college, can't get pregnant, were fired from your job, or were diagnosed with cancer, chances are you experienced—or are experiencing—some sort of shame about it. Maybe you felt that your peers would judge you or that your parents would be disappointed in you or that your coworkers would treat you differently. Being concerned about what others think of you doesn't make you crazy. We all do it. But if you want to do the best you can to move yourself through the painful transition of change and into the next phase of life, you have to openly accept whatever it is that has happened as reality. This starts with accepting and honoring the change as a part of your life now.

When change hurts, the medicine that will make you feel better is actually quite simple: you must take your power back. Be bold. You are the only one who truly knows what is right for you. Society may say that it is not "normal" for a single woman to have a baby, or they may tell you that it is not "normal" to love somebody of the same sex. The list can go on and on. Is it "normal" to break an engagement? Or leave a high-paying job because you aren't happy? You are the one who decides what works for you. Who says divorce can't be a huge blessing? If you were married to the wrong person, someone who made you deeply unhappy and insecure, then it most certainly is. The more confidently you accept the change, the more those around you will accept you for who you are and the decisions you make.

Accepting the Positive Changes

Difficult changes aren't the only changes that are hard to accept. Positive changes can also be intimidating and anxiety provoking. If something good happens, we may fear that the change won't last or that somehow we aren't worthy of it. Or maybe we fear that we will be unable to live up to the new responsibility that comes with the change. Or we may not have been expecting this change, and the surprise of it is too much to bear. But mostly we feel that we have no control over what, exactly, this new good thing may mean, or how people will view us now.

A new positive change can often take something away, so there may also be some feeling of emptiness. And a positive change often requires work. That's also why some of us are hesitant to pursue changes that will enhance our lives. We might want to lose weight, but we do nothing about it for fear that the loss will be short-lived. And if we do lose it all, we worry that we won't be able to maintain our new weight. If we suddenly made money, we fear that our friends would be jealous. If we stopped being unhappy, perhaps we would miss the support we get from so many people. If we had a baby, we'd have to work to be a good parent, and we'd have to make sacrifices. So we sabotage and resist the positive changes, too. We fall back on old patterns and the familiar. When we're in that space, at least we know how we fit in.

A change optimist always remembers to accept himself or herself. You must accept that you need to be your own best friend and be kind and gentle to yourself while moving through change. Beating yourself up is counterproductive to healthy change. You are allowed—encouraged, actually—to treat yourself with love and respect.

Ask yourself, *Am I being good to myself? Am I allowing this change to happen?*

Helping a Friend Through Change

Sometimes we also need to accept our friends' changes. Often we don't realize how we are reacting to their situation, because our intentions are good. The famous dancer Isadora Duncan had a young son and daughter who, tragically, were killed when her chauffer got into a car accident. After it happened, Isadora's pain became unbearable and she simply could not deal with the loss or accept what had happened. All she could do was talk about them: their smiles, their favorite foods, and their favorite things. Her friends didn't know how to help her through this period, so they tried to change the subject. They tried to distract her, taking her to new places and lightening up the conversation if it got too gloomy. None of this made Isadora feel any better.

One weekend, Isadora was invited to Italy by a friend she hadn't seen since the tragic loss. This friend did something very different: she asked Isadora to tell her everything about her kids—all the pain, all the memories, all the feelings she had. Her friend didn't try to change the subject; she listened and she cried. She focused on just 'being' with her. And Isadora felt her pain lighten for the first time ever. Why? Finally someone had been able to fully feel, listen to, and accept all of her pain and emotions. This allowed her to begin to move through what had happened.

When you are being a friend to someone, often you are helping him or her through change. Remember this while you work to help friends in need: if you accept what it is they are saying, they will feel heard and understood. Only then will you have the ability to guide them, to help them find their way, and to lift them up. But acceptance is not the same thing as agreeing. I can accept that a friend feels insecure; I can accept that a friend feels lonely; I can accept that someone has given up on God. But this does not mean that I agree with what he or she is feeling. Simply accepting his or her pain, fear, or other emotion is sufficient to help. They will feel heard.

The Optimist's Mind-Set: Leave the Past Behind

As we learned earlier, whether the change is positive, like getting married or having a baby—or more difficult, like being treated for a disease—it's important that we learn to let go of old ways of being and living. This is not always easy. Anything we let go of will involve a sense of loss and confusion, of being between two worlds. We may feel displaced, as if we are going nowhere.

Letting go can be incredibly challenging, because the controller in us craves certainty. It says, "I have no time for letting go." But if you let go of the need to control the outcome of any given situation, you will significantly reduce the pain you feel and will be one step closer to accepting the change as reality. I like to look at change as an invitation to see what will happen next. It's like watching a performance and wondering who or what will appear from behind the curtain. Learn to live with anticipation instead of fear.

Abby maintains that when she was diagnosed with breast cancer, one of the hardest things for her to let go of was not the idea that she was guaranteed a long, healthy life, but the belief that she would always have her thick, beautiful hair. "Once I accepted the fact that I was going to lose all of my hair in chemotherapy, my biggest concern was about how others would react to my baldness. I didn't want my friends to feel uncomfortable seeing me without hair. I wanted to be sure they knew that I was cool with it, and that they should be, too. I needed them to feel as natural about my being bald as I did," she says. Abby decided that the easiest way to accomplish this was to involve her friends in the process. To do this, she threw a haircutting party after her first chemo treatment. It was the ultimate letting-go party. Each friend cut a handful of her hair, and to lighten the mood, they each tied a group of strands with a pink ribbon, and everyone kept one. "This made them see how bizarre the whole situation was, and made them all realize that I could see some humor in my plight. It loosened everyone up. They realized they could talk openly to me about the cancer, and they have felt that way ever since. Everyone accepted the change I was experiencing."

> **Surrender to the mind**
> **of the Universe.**
> **—Deepak Chopra**

We are so used to struggling that if we didn't, it would feel strange. But keep in mind that the absence of struggle is grace. Accepting a change does not mean sitting on the couch, drinking excessively, or watching too much TV. Instead, it's allowing yourself to move with the current of life, to go willingly where it wants to take you.

Lisa had always dreamed of being a grandmother. She had three daughters and was excited to see them get married and have children. At the age of nineteen, her eldest daughter became pregnant. She had just started college. She decided to keep the baby, and her mother fully supported her decision. They shared the moments of pregnancy together with love, excitement, and fun. Then, her daughter made a drastic decision a few weeks before her due date. She would give the baby girl up for adoption. Lisa describes the moment as "the most excruciating pain I have ever felt. There was no way I could change her decision. I was not in control." The little girl, her first and only grandchild, was given to another family. It took Lisa years to accept what happened and to see the good in it. Today her daughter is thirty-six, not married, has no other children, and is at peace with the decision she made many years ago. Lisa's other daughters do not have kids either, and she has learned to accept the direction that her children's lives have taken. "I've gone through a radical acceptance that my children's lives are not mine to control, that people make their own choices, and that any more resistance to the adoption would have probably made me ill," she says.

Asking why something happened is a red light to accepting change, while asking "What for" is a green light to accept and move forward.

While you are in the midst of change, allow yourself to fully feel whatever it is that comes up. Let the questions, suffering, shock, fear, and anger move through you. Cry the tears, whether they are tears of sadness, frustration, joy, or gratitude. Shout out the words *This is so unfair, this is so hard.* Write down your feelings. Talk to friends, loved ones, or a professional. What you're feeling is completely natural. It's OK. Everyone else feels emotions like this, and they *will* subside. Accept the turbulence on the river. No one said it wouldn't be a bumpy ride sometimes. Just point your boat in the direction of the current, so the energy of life is with you and not against you, and things will get better.

☑ Take Action

1. What is the one thing you know you must accept? The aspect of your life that still brings up much resistance?

2. Write down a couple of other life situations, changes that you still refuse to accept. They could have happened many years ago, to you or to someone close to you. Maybe you found out that your son is gay, maybe you had an affair or are struggling with an addiction, maybe someone did something to you, or maybe you made a terrible mistake.

3. Write down something that you used to struggle to accept but that today you are at peace with—perhaps getting divorced, being in debt, or having an abortion.

4. How did you find peace and accept this situation? How can you do the same with the changes you identified above?

5. Examine what you did to help turn your boat around and accept a situation that was originally hard.

The final part of accepting a change is to remember the change guarantee and to believe that something good will come from this situation. Understanding that life is on your side and having faith that your higher self is leading you on the right path will guide you to complete acceptance. If you resist the change, you will lose 100 percent of the time. The sooner you accept that something has changed, the sooner you will move through it and onto the next phase of life. Acceptance never means forgetting or minimizing, but choosing to move forward. It's often the hardest thing to simply accept what is, but it can bring about the biggest relief and freedom from a situation. The best healing is to surrender and then watch what life brings to you.

When you take the time to really accept and acknowledge the changes in your life, you will be able to use the change GPS by formulating a clear understanding of where you are now and where you want to go in the near future. Resistance stops you from moving forward. It's like trying to drive with the parking brake activated.

The first thirty days are the relief moment, the letting-go moment, the time when you lift the brake, when you are ready to let the change be as it is and allow the transformation to begin.

> *The first step toward change is acceptance. Once you accept yourself, you open the door to change. That's all you have to do. Change is not something you do, it's something you allow.*
> *—Will Garcia,*
>   *AIDS patient*

The First 30 Days: What to Remember

1. Resisting change is what causes so much pain.

2. Accepting change puts you back in the right direction. Align your boat with the current of the river, let go, and be open to the journey—the bumps *and* the calmness that will eventually come.

3. The sooner you allow life to carry you, the better you will feel.

6 The Things You *Can* Control

What You Say, Think, and Feel

> **Principle 6: People who successfully navigate change use empowering questions and words, think better thoughts, and express their feelings.**
>
> *At your most stuck point, if you can speak with different words, think a slightly better thought, and get in touch with how you are feeling, you can become unstuck in a matter of minutes.*

Change can make you feel out of control. If you're debating whether to initiate a change, or if you're right in the middle of a change that life has handed you, it's natural to feel lost as you look for certainty (that everything is going to be OK), clarity (what's the next best step to make?), and reassurance (that you will eventually feel better).

Though you can't control how or when things change, there are a few key factors that you *can* control: the words you say, the dominant thoughts you have, and the feelings you allow yourself to feel. These things can make your change more difficult, or they can spark momentum, hope, and optimism. This simple shift can have a dramatic effect on how you feel while going through change, especially in the first thirty days. When you stop trying to control your circumstances and work instead on controlling what goes on inside of you, you will find that you encounter less pain and suffering and more acceptance and relief. When we start to feel better on the inside, our outside conditions will soon improve as well, but we often want outside conditions to change *before* we feel better.

These are the things you can control . . .

The Language You Use

The Words You Choose

Start observing the words and language you use to describe the change you're going through. Act like a teacher who is listening for correct grammar and vocabulary. Do you exaggerate, do you speak like a victim, or do you swear a lot? When we are in the chaos of change, we nearly all exaggerate and go to extremes, saying things like "This has been the worst day of my life" or "I've never been so depressed."

Imagine that you are describing a change to a friend. Notice the language you choose when recounting a recent health diagnosis, breakup, or trouble at work. Say it out loud; don't worry, nobody's listening. Now practice describing the situation again, this time using language that embraces the positives of your new circumstances. Yes, there are *always* positives.

Two approaches to language—from somebody who was recently fired

> *A) Today was the worst day of my life. I was asked to leave my job. I had been there for ten years and had helped the company grow to where it is today. I gave everything to that place. I can't believe they did this to me. I am so angry and pissed off. And what am I supposed to tell people now? I'm ashamed to be out of work and don't know what I'm going to do next. This is an absolute nightmare.*

> *B) Today I was asked to leave my job. I had been there for ten years and had helped the company grow. I am sad to leave, but also excited to see what's next for me. I gave them everything, and now its time to give my energy to other things. I'm looking forward to having more time for my husband and daughter. I'm also going to go to the gym and finally get in shape. There are so many things I have wanted to try, and now I can. I'm excited—and also a little anxious.*

Can you see the difference between these two accounts? The second example may seem unnatural and forced—not an honest representation of how somebody in the middle of a difficult change would really feel. But when you shift your language to the positive, you will start to believe what you say, and your life will begin moving in a better direction. When you speak about your change in a negative manner, you risk becoming imprisoned in a pessimistic spiral of words and creating a life that mirrors that feeling. Yes, change is already challenging, but if you can make the additional effort to reshape the way you describe what you are going through, you will start to feel lighter and more optimistic.

Change one negative word that you always seem to fall back on. I always catch people using negative words such as *crisis, suffering, disaster,* and *impossible.* Words like these literally keep us trapped by not leaving room for a solution to come forward.

Now is the perfect moment to start recognizing your language patterns. Listen closely to what you say to yourself and to others. Is it freeing you or keeping you locked in a box?

When change is afoot, we have plenty of opportunities to tell people about what has happened to us or about the difficulty of the change we are making. But often we rehash the same story, make the same excuses, and express the same sadness and bitterness. We even add gruesome details, just to make our story more interesting. Remember when you were dumped? Or when the tough new boss arrived at your job? Or when your latest diet failed? Think of the extra story lines you created or the subtext you added just to heighten the drama and justify your position.

> *For me, words are a form of action, capable of influencing change.*
> —*Ingrid Bengis*

Language may seem like a minor thing while we're going through change, but the words we choose can blind us to the reality of what is really happening. I call these blinding words *victim vocabulary.* You are what you say and what you tell people, and if you choose words of oppression over words of opportunity, that will be how you experience change. Have you ever found yourself saying anything like the following?

I wouldn't have been fired if my boss wasn't such a jerk.

The only reason we broke up is because she was crazy.

I am not in a relationship now because I am a single mother over forty.

I can't find a job because I'm too old.

My body won't let go of this extra weight.

This is victim vocabulary at work.

Recently, as I was helping my friend Kathy through cancer, I noticed that she was using some very negative words and expressing many negative emotions in describing the progression of her disease. She had locked herself into one version of how she first became sick, when she discovered the tumor, what the doctors said, and who was to blame. To shift her language patterns, I asked her to practice speaking only of what she wanted in her life from this point on, not where she had come from. I introduced her to the change GPS and the only two questions that matter: Where are you now? Where do you want to go? Navigators have no interest in where you were yesterday. Kathy now speaks only of what she is creating and moving toward. She doesn't have to relive the same story— and all the negative emotions that accompany it—every time she talks about her illness. Instead, by speaking only of forward momentum, she engages the positive emotions and hope that surround a new and exciting future. Remember, repeating an old

> *Watch your thoughts, for they become words. Watch your words, for they become actions. Watch your actions, for they become habits. Watch your habits, for they become character. Watch your character, for it becomes your destiny.*
> *—Anonymous*

story keeps it stuck in your mind, body, and soul. And the First 30 Days is about moving forward, not staying stuck.

You can practice releasing victim vocabulary by having the courage to tell the story of your change with less emotion. When recounting what has happened, pretend you're a journalist, and stick to only the facts. A journalist has to check his facts, over and over, ensuring that every point is real and not an assumption. A journalist also makes sure that each story detail exists in the present and that he or she isn't speculating about what could happen in the future. When recounting your change, stick with what you know to be 100 percent true.

People have a few words that they always use. Think about some of your close friends or colleagues: what words do you identify them with? Do they use the word *awesome* or *fabulous*? Or, on the negative side, do they overuse the word *awful* or *disaster*? What are the words that you always opt for? It's time to be pickier about these, too.

The Questions You Ask Yourself

When change is present, we also become experts at asking ourselves disempowering questions:

Why did this happen to me?

How could I have been so stupid or blind or crazy?

How long is this going to last?

Will I ever feel calm and happy again?

Will this ever end?

And if it's a positive change:

Am I good enough for something like this?

Will I fail or mess this up?

Questions That Will Empower You and Make Change Easier

What could be great about this change?

Will I allow myself to be empowered by this or diminished?

How long will I allow my life to be on hold before I surrender to what is happening?

Could this change be protecting me from something?

What opportunity has this change brought to me?

Can I find some humor in this?

What part of my life can I focus on that hasn't changed?

Who can help me?

What can I focus on now?

What steps must I take now?

How am I succeeding right now?

What can I be grateful for?

What was great about today?

What have I already accomplished?

How can I reward myself and celebrate my progress so far?

Write these questions down, keep them in your pocket or purse, and answer them daily. You can either set a fixed time to do this each day or pick them up whenever you need them most. When we ask the right questions, we begin to see a gift and opportunity in change. Change becomes a new way of approaching life.

We're quick to rattle off the negative questions, but here's a question we probably don't ask ourselves enough: *What is the positive lesson I can learn from this change?* At first, your mind might react strongly against this question, but keep gently pushing yourself for answers, and allow them to take root inside of you. Changing the meaning that you give to these transitions will liberate you from your past and open you to your future.

The Stories You Tell

We all come up with reasons for why something happened or is not happening in our lives. Often, they are born from assumptions, projections, fear, and hypotheses. We have told our stories dozens of times to the people in our lives. Repeating a story over and over gives us relief because it is familiar, comfortable, expected, and helps us get attention and support from others. We cling to our story like a life vest: it keeps us afloat and allows us to justify anything and everything.

I was recently sharing with a friend about how difficult it is to be single in New York. I was telling her how I didn't enjoy the dating scene and that there weren't any men in New York who wanted a relationship and that I was sad and struggled with this. I spoke for about ten minutes before she said, "You know, I hear what you're saying, and that's your story, but I am not going to listen to it anymore. Your story is not real. It has you going around in the same circle, where you always see the same perspective." I realized two things then. First, a real friend will stop your pattern of negative language. Second, I had been boring people with this same story for years! So I decided to let my story go for just two weeks, and guess what? I immediately went on a couple of dates.

My dating story got me thinking of all the other stories I habitually pull out, like familiar books in a library. There's the story about my childhood, the story about my business, the story about my finances, about my parents' divorce—it was quite amazing to see how many tales I had gathered. These stories defined me because I recounted them as fact. And now I made a commitment to catch myself when I started telling any of my stories again. The next time I felt a story coming on, I would choose instead to be quiet, which would create space for something new, something life had not yet revealed to me.

When you cling to the story of why you are sick, why you are fat, why you are broke, why you are not working, why you haven't spoken to your mom or dad, or why you haven't changed jobs or moved, the story becomes your excuse for not taking action. The story allows you to be a victim of circumstance and stops any forward momentum by freezing the situation in place.

I recently met a woman who kept repeating the same story: "In the last two years I have put on twenty-five pounds." I kept hearing this story, and eventually I asked her for permission to share some coaching and feedback. I pointed out to her how familiar that statement had become for her, how it was like a security blanket, something she held on to. I asked her to not speak that sentence to anyone at any time, ever again. And if she did unwittingly speak it, she was to imagine gaining one pound each time. That was the weight of the story! From here on, when discussing her weight, she would say only: "I am now living a healthy life, eating right, and exercising." By activating her internal GPS system, she would be able to see where she is today and where she wants to go tomorrow. After just one month of using this new language, she lost seven pounds. So don't allow your story to become your crutch, your excuse to stay stuck. It's time to create a new story, one with a better ending. This requires an initial leap of faith to see another possible reality.

 # Take Action

Write down the stories you tell the most.

1. Think of the tales you tell about the people in your life: your mom, dad, siblings, spouse, ex-lovers, bosses, and friends.

2. What are the stories you tell about yourself? (I am depressed, too old, bad with money, etc.)

3. Think of the stories you tell about changes that didn't feel good at the time: a break-up, a job loss, a rejection of some sort, an illness, or a bad decision.

4. Write down the stories you tell about changes you are currently experiencing and changes you have yet to make and commit to stop telling them. Make a decision.

When you feel an old story coming on, stop it in its tracks by saying, *You know, I used to have a whole story that justified this, but I don't anymore.* Notice how good it feels to take your power back from the story and the negative thoughts that have been ruling that area of your life.

Affirmations

Affirmations are word patterns, sentences, and phrases that replace the negative things we say to ourselves. The act of stating something in the positive and then repeating it triggers the brain to think differently about something. Most of us have at least one negative loop in our heads: *I always screw up. I am not smart. I never get it right. I am fat. I am old. I am worthless. Nobody loves me. I can't change. I'm not a businessperson. I'm terrible with money.*

These are the lies we tell ourselves, the junk we feed our minds. We all know about junk food, but junk thoughts are even more toxic. The way you feel about yourself radiates from your thoughts whether you recognize it or not, so start thinking good things about who you are.

Affirmations are very simple. They need to be stated in the present, in the positive, and they need to be repeated often. If you want to lose weight, tell yourself: *I am in perfect health and physically fit today.* If you want to attract a great relationship, tell yourself: *Life is bringing me my soul mate today.* It's important to write your affirmation down every morning and every evening, because the act of writing helps you focus.

✓ Take Action

Write an affirmation about an area of your life that you want to change, like your career or your health. This phrase will become your mantra— something that will trigger your body and mind to start believing. Write it down in visible places and start saying it as you make breakfast, when you are driving, or while you are taking a shower. Believe that it is true. If you're committed to affecting change in your life, take a few moments to do this exercise everyday. The results can be powerful.

What You Think

Positive Thoughts: Make Them Work for You

When you change the way you think, you tap into your inner voice and become an award-winning film director. You control the movies in your mind. You can make them bright, dark, negative, lonely, or uplifting. Remember, you see these films over and over again, so they can have a huge impact on what shows up in your life.

I learned the power of these "movies in my mind" when I recently ran the New York City Marathon. I always try to run the marathon with a disabled runner. This often involves walking or running slowly for several hours and making sure my companion is OK on every level. Over the years, I have accompanied a blind runner, a woman in a wheelchair, someone with MS, and someone who was mentally handicapped. I never know who I am going to share those 26.2 miles with or how long it will take until a few days before.

Last year, life had some fun in store for me when I met my running partner, Sven, a runner from Norway with cystic fibrosis. I asked him how long he thought it would take him to run the marathon, and he proudly declared his goal: five hours! The one year when I had trained fully, I completed the marathon in about five hours. But this year I had not run more than five miles at a time. This worried me. Without training, I thought, there is no way I can run the race successfully with Sven. I tried to assign a different volunteer to him, but when that didn't work, I decided to go with the flow. The next morning, as I found myself at the starting line, some pretty negative thoughts and images—my movies—tried to make their way into my head. I feared that I would get hurt soon in the race, I imagined the shame of having to drop out, and I was worried that I would disappoint Sven. I then realized that I had a choice: I could continue with this stream of negative thoughts, or I could shift the way I was thinking. I decided to think one thought: *My body will surprise me in a good way.* And then I was off. Twenty-six miles later I crossed the finish line, completing the race in about five hours and thirty minutes. Shockingly, I wasn't too sore and had no cramps. Sven was an inspiration to me. His determination and humor helped us both cross the finish line. Throughout the race, I never allowed myself to think a thought that would give my body an excuse to stop or get hurt. The marathon is a physical endurance test, but on that November day I personally tested the power of my thoughts; it was much more of a thinking endurance test.

Changes always involve a lot of thinking—too much thinking, in fact. Our brain tries to figure it all out: the why, the how, the when. Sometimes we need to just turn off the thinking switch. I haven't figured out how to shut down all thoughts, but I have found that you can choose a positive pattern of thinking. But first you have to acknowledge the negative thoughts that are running through your mind.

My friend Ann is a change hero. She activated the power of positive thinking as she moved through a series of very painful changes. If you met her today, you would never know what she has experienced. After college Ann was misdiagnosed with a life-threatening illness, and she believed her life would soon end. She saw numerous doctors and spent time in many hospitals; her family spent large amounts of money trying to find a cure. Then catastrophe turned into her greatest blessing as she began to "think differently and live each day as if it were my last." Inspired, she moved to Mexico, where she was enjoying life until she was brutally mugged and left roadside to die. "During the mugging, I somehow had the ability to feel and express love to my assailant," Ann says. "I'm convinced to this day that the thought of compassion is what saved my life."

After surviving those two extremely difficult changes, Ann fell happily in love. But she faced change once again when her fiancé fell off of a horse and died very suddenly. After many months of grieving, she returned to New York, started a new job, and eventually fell in love again. But there were still more changes in store. On September 11, 2001, her second fiancé and several of his coworkers died in the attacks on the World Trade Center. "He left me a voice mail that morning saying good-bye and asking me to live the best life possible. But it was difficult to listen to his plea, and I tried to fill the emptiness I felt with food, men, work, and materialistic things, but nothing seemed to make the pain go away," she says. "Finally, I made the decision to accept what had happened and fill the void with positive thoughts of myself and my future. It had been my fiancé's last wish. Throughout each transition, no matter how painful, I always continued to believe good thoughts." Today Ann, at the age of thirty-four, is happily married to a wonderful man (they skipped the engagement part), has gone back to school to pursue a PhD, and never recounts negatives stories of her past changes.

> *Our strongest currency is our thoughts.*
> *—Wayne Dyer*

Changing Your Expectations

When working to control your thoughts, it helps to acknowledge your expectations. There is a direct link between the expectations we have and how easily we get through change. Expectations cast a spell on us. We think one way is the right way, and it subsequently freezes out any other ways of being. We don't allow life to do its thing, to reveal what is intended.

Expectations show up strongest during the first thirty days, when we are still hooked on how things should be, what should have happened. Then, over time, we see how futile it is to impose what our mind thinks on life. Life will do its thing with or without our mind's participation. We need to transform fear into hope and let go of our expectations of how a change will develop.

When change shows up, or you believe you are ready to make a change, step aside and ask yourself immediately, *What do I expect here?* Take a moment to bring all of your expectations into the light. Do you expect the change to be hard? Do you expect it to take forever? Do you expect to be the one who loses out? Do you expect to feel alone and excluded? Do you have such a specific vision of how something will go that you will be disappointed when it turns out differently? Or, do you expect this to be the very best day of your life?

Do you see how hard you are setting things up to be, often before you have even started to make a change?

Marie, another woman I know, acknowledged her expectations when she met an amazing guy and waited for him to get in touch. When he didn't call or write she went through a lot of pain, because she expected that he would. She came up with a host of negative thoughts to justify his lack of communication— reasons she was unlikable or things she had said or done when they met. She stopped any other possibility from showing up by going against the flow of the river and deciding how things were supposed to unfold—he was *supposed* to call—instead of allowing life to happen as it needed to. As soon as she realized she had piled expectations on the situation, life brought a few other men to her attention, and her little obsession with the first quickly vanished.

Choose to Be an Eagle, Not a Duck

Someone I met on a trip recently shared the following expression: "You can't send ducks to eagle school." I just love this phrase! Think about these two birds for a minute. How do they behave differently?

Ducks . . .

. . . feel powerless.

. . . act like the victim.

. . . believe they can't rise above something.

. . . do what everyone else does (hang around the tribe).

. . . quack (talk) a lot.

. . . congregate in groups.

. . . are quick and reactive.

. . . can't be alone.

Eagles . . .

. . . feel powerful.

. . . soar above emotions and turmoil.

Canceling Negative Thoughts

A friend of mine says, "Cancel, cancel" when consciously stopping negative thoughts, ideas, and pictures from taking over his mind. I practiced this recently when I was out running. I had the negative thought that a truck would hit me, and before my imagination could get a grip on that image—creating the movie in my mind—I immediately said, "Cancel, cancel." When a negative thought comes into your mind, see it, erase it, and then replace it with one that is more helpful. During the first thirty days of

. . . don't follow the rules.

. . . are resourceful.

. . . do things differently.

. . . have high standards.

. . . rely on all types of help and resources; without the wind's resistance, eagles would fall flat on their faces.

. . . take their time to decide what to do next.

. . . don't always need to know exactly where they are going.

. . . can be alone for a while.

Ask yourself one simple question: *Am I thinking duck thoughts or eagle thoughts?* A friend of mine has become so hooked on thinking eagle thoughts that he bought a six-foot photograph of an eagle to put in his home. Simply adding a new image for his brain to focus on and think about during a time of change has made his transitions less challenging. When he messes up, he even says, "That was duck behavior."

change, your thoughts will throw several "negativity parties" in your head. Develop the "Cancel, cancel" habit—or "erase and replace"—to quiet these down.

☑️ Take Action

1. Use the first thirty days to practice thinking better thoughts. Start with just twenty-four hours of catching yourself with negative (duck) thoughts and replacing them with positive (eagle) ones.

Do you think you'll never get healthier, never lose weight, never get through the next month, never get married, never have any money?

2. Ask your friends what it is you often say that holds you back. They will know very clearly what negative thoughts you are stuck on. Listen to them, and then reach for a better thought. Once you've gotten used to thinking more positive thoughts for twenty-four hours, move up to three days, one week, and so forth. We all have the strength to shift our thoughts toward the positive, but it requires us to engage our change muscle and to be patient and gentle with ourselves.

What You Feel

Though they can be painful, many challenging emotions and feelings are actually working to help you through change. Too many times we equate negative feelings with something terrible. We think we must be doing something wrong if we feel sad or frustrated or angry. But remember, as we learned with the change demons, your feelings are your compass, your indicator, your pointer toward that which needs to change to help you feel better. Your feelings are gifts. Thank them, welcome them, and ask them to turn up the volume. The negative feelings should be welcomed even more than the happy ones, because they carry more indicators of where you need to be heading.

Grieving the Old and Welcoming the New:
Don't Deny the Darkness or It Will Show Up Again

An enlightened master once said that there is no grief that cannot be finished in seven days' time *if* you can sit in the fire of it and feel it fully. But we typically run from the grieving stage of change. Remember that loss is a part of every change. Think about it: even good changes involve loss in some way—having a baby, getting married, becoming famous, succeeding at work or in a new business, going back to college, making money. Look deeply within yourself and ask: *What do I feel I am losing with the change I am experiencing today?* Freedom, money, status, friendship, youth, health, excitement, love, affection? There is only one way to move through grief, and that is by grieving.

Now ask yourself: *What am I gaining?* When life takes something from you, it always gives you something in return. It is normal to grieve what you have lost, but you must also eventually welcome what you may have gained. Grieving doesn't cause a past situation to turn out any differently. Grieving is for you, and you only. It's your medicine. Take it for as long as you need. If you are getting married, grieve your single years and then focus on what to embrace in your new life. If you are retiring, grieve your working years and then get happy and focus on all the possibilities that are available to you now.

If you are going through a change and are not feeling the loss of something, you are probably in denial. Being able to grieve is a sign of confidence, not weakness. You grieve knowing full well that your grief, like everything else in life, will change and transform. When we are in the middle of it, though, it feels permanent.

Although Martin's father was diagnosed with multiple myeloma almost ten years prior to his death, it was still impossible for Martin to prepare for the grief he would feel once his dad passed away. "I don't think any of us believe our parents or spouses will leave us one day, even though we know beyond any doubt that it will happen," he says. "The shock I felt soon turned to anger and rage at God for basically maintaining the order of life and death.

It doesn't seem fair that people have to leave before they are ready or before those around are ready to let them go."

Martin soon moved into a phase of severe loneliness. And then things began to shift. "Each day the 'missing' lessened and I was comforted by all the things I still had. I also realized that my mother needed help that only my brothers and I could give her and also that other people around me—my fiancée, my nieces, nephews, and coworkers—needed me to be a man like my father was. I came through this difficult experience by allowing myself to feel whatever it was that I was feeling and turning to others for support and guidance."

> *Joy and sorrow are inseparable . . . together they come and when one sits alone with you . . . remember that the other is asleep upon your bed.*
> *—Kahlil Gibran*

As Cynthia discovered, grieving is also present during very exciting and positive changes. As she prepared to leave New York after ten years of living there, she felt a real loss. "This was a very strange emotion as I was moving cross-country to go live with my fiancé, a really happy occasion," she says. She packed and then had a going-away party with all of her friends, but through it all she would often break into tears. "Nothing was wrong with my future. What felt sad was leaving behind a city I loved and a comfortable and habitual way of living." Cynthia realized that she needed to grieve her years in New York before she would be able to embrace her new life. A couple of weeks later the loss began to fade. "It was a good thing that I let myself feel the sadness. There was no way I could have pretended to be completely joyful at the beginning of my life in this new city."

So let the tears flow if they need to; release the emotion, the tension, and the stress. If you do it now, you won't be as distraught when you think back on this loss or when someone brings it up later. For example, if you lost a parent and didn't fully feel that experience when it happened, whenever you hear of someone else going through the same experience or even someone referring to a parent, your loss will be triggered. It's like a lover from an unresolved relationship who keeps appearing in your life. All the pain and memories come flooding back. Even if you're happy about a change in your life—such as getting divorced—you still need to grieve what was. It's the same with starting college and being away from home, or giving birth and leaving behind a youthful way of life. Allow your body, mind, and heart to let you know what they feel they have lost. Identify the feelings. You will already have stripped the emotions of some power if you claim them from the lost-and-found bin.

The Snap Point

There is a point that we all come to where we realize that we absolutely must change, and that we will survive when we do. This point can come when something continually feels off or when something keeps calling you to change. It's that moment when you say, *Enough, no more, that's it.* Your snap point can be triggered by the needs of a loved one, your health, or the future of your business. The birth of your first child may be the snap point for you to finally quit smoking; the threat of losing your spouse may be the snap point for you to start communicating more openly and to be more kind and patient. Coming to your snap point will supercharge your change muscle, your feelings of worthiness, and your ability to handle anything. This is the part of you that says: *Yes, give it to me. I can handle it. I feel strong and capable. I will not give up.* It's like an elastic band—hence the word *snap*. Once it has been stretched to its furthest point, it snaps. That's it—done, can't go back to what it was!

Sometimes we give up on change. We may think that one of our parents is never going to change, and in doing so we have learned to live with a strained relationship. Or we think we will never change our body because we have tried a hundred times before. Ask yourself where you have given up, or ask your friends where they think you have given up. Very often, the areas that we want and need to change the most are the areas that seem the most overwhelming to change, and so we are hesitant to tackle them. It's never too late to change.

I asked several people what their snap point was, what happened that finally made them decide to change, the moment when they said, *Enough, no more!*

My friend Doris had been a smoker for seventeen years, and after she had tried to quit several times, one of her friends showed her another way to kick-start the change—by focusing on something different. She reminded Doris that she had always striven to be a role model for strong, healthy women looking to pursue their dreams and that smoking didn't fit in with the identity she was working to create. How could she possibly be a role model and a smoker at the same time? And that was it. Doris hasn't smoked since.

Another person, Mike, told me he finally decided to sell his family business when his girlfriend pointed out just how disconnected he had become from her and their new baby. She expressed her feelings about the pain it was creating for her with such gentleness and honesty that it inspired Mike to make the decision to sell the business.

Liz told me how her husband's genuine concern was the catalyst that encouraged her to seek help for her alcoholism. He asked her to come with him to AA meetings in order to save their marriage. When she saw the pain and worry in his eyes, she accepted his invitation and has now been sober for fourteen years.

As you can see from these examples, the snap point is often associated with a feeling of pain—usually the pain of hurting someone else, of hating a part of your life, of living with your fears, or of feeling ashamed of who you are becoming.

Keep in mind that the pace at which your life transforms is directly related to the way you react to change. Your language, thoughts, and feelings are three things you can control during the uncertain time of change. It takes effort and patience to switch your habitual way of speaking, thinking, and feeling to better, brighter words, thoughts, and emotions. One better question, one decision, or one new choice can be the answer to creating change. Start today, and you will be on the way to a much more optimistic view of navigating change and navigating life.

The First 30 Days: What to Remember

1. Be very mindful of the questions you ask yourself, the language and words that you use, and the stories that you tell. They can imprison or liberate you during change.

2. You can control your thoughts during change. Choose the good ones. Reach for a better thought, always.

3. All changes involve a loss, and it's OK to feel the emotions that accompany that loss. Some level of pain will often serve you and may bring you to your snap point, where you finally initiate a change.

7 Meet Your Spiritual Side

Where Tranquility, Ideas, and Wisdom Live

Principle 7: People who successfully navigate change know they are connected to something bigger than themselves.

When everything around you is changing, look for the part of you that doesn't change. The part that is calm, centered, and always there.

In this chapter I'm not going to tell you who or what to believe in or what to call God. You are not going to have to change any of your personal beliefs around faith, religion, or traditions. But I am going to ask you to establish a stronger, deeper relationship with the *real you*—the calm, centered secure part of you—while letting your tired and scared mind take a rest.

When we make a change in our lives—going back to school, starting a business, pursuing a creative path—we also provoke an identity shift. And even though the changes are external, often it's more of an internal journey that we are being asked to take. To ensure that we don't get lost along the way, we need to connect with the core of our being, the essence of who we are.

Every great leader, athlete, and hero has believed in something greater than himself or herself. Nelson Mandela, Gandhi, Mother Theresa, and JFK are among the many who referred to a connection with something greater: their soul, their source, or their relationship to God or the Divine. They acknowledged the presence of the Divine in every difficult situation, and they allowed it to be a helping presence in their lives. During the first thirty days of moving through a change, and throughout your whole life, it's important to ask yourself what you are willing to trust. Really ask yourself, *Where is my trust these days?*

> *If you don't like the phrase higher self, call it something else. Whatever the label, it's the part of you that makes you feel good when you don't react out of anger, fear, impatience, or blame. It lets you know you've taken the high road.*

Some of us believe there is something bigger going on. We look at nature, at the miracle of birth, a sunrise, the stars above, and contemplate a bigger sense of power, a feeling that we are not alone, that something—or someone—is present. This something is the sanctuary that can help us get centered in times of crisis and change. We may not know this for sure, but maybe there is some sort of energy, a power we can tap into, an army of invisible forces just waiting to help us. Perhaps they exist solely to assist us, to prepare the way, and to be on our side. I call them *my friends upstairs.*

We all have things we turn to. Perhaps it's meditation, prayer, a belief in the law of attraction, or visualization. Or maybe it's a connection to nature, a certain type of calming music, or a cre-

Connect, Reconnect, and Remain Connected

Many of us have strong religious beliefs and would say we are very connected to a bigger force. Some of us have a more general spiritual outlook, and some of us don't know what to believe anymore. Whatever it is for you, you can choose to tune in to this broader energy—what may be called God, Allah, Buddha, Jesus, Krishna, or Rama, among other names, or just simply nature—every single day by focusing inward and noticing how things feel. You can access this energy in many ways: you can take a quiet walk, sit in silence, pray, express your gratitude, read a helpful book, or meditate. Just take a few minutes and go inside. It is always present. Once you become attuned to it, you can feel its stability, guidance, and gentle suggestions.

ative outlet like writing or painting. Whatever it is, it will help you during times of change by allowing you to connect to who you really are.

Even during the most dramatic change, there is always a place within us that is calm, collected, and comfortable, that knows how to cope with change. This part of ourselves doesn't fluctuate when circumstances are changing all around us. For most of us, it's something we call our higher self, our soul, or our connection to the Divine or God.

During times of change, most of us crave understanding. We want to make sense of the seeming chaos around us. The place I'm speaking of, though, I call *inner-standing*. It's the part of you that is calm and wise, that accepts things as they are. That part of you is eternal, unchanging; it is whole and complete, and you can't get rid of it no matter how hard you try. Connecting to this inner place means aligning with the person you were before the change, during the change, and after the change. It's about remembering who you are.

Peace and Quiet

No matter what change or transition is going on, no matter what decision you need to make, find some time to be alone and silent. Often we are looking for more peace in our lives, but we don't do what we need to do to make it happen. So many times our higher self tries to give us answers or solutions, but with all our busyness, we can never stop to reflect. This is why meditation has become so popular in our culture today. Although you may think of meditation as passive, it is in fact an active way of creating time in the day to connect with the deeper part of yourself. Meditation stops your resistance to change by allowing you to find the relationship between the little you and the bigger you and to remind yourself that you are exactly where you need to be. When you get quiet you'll see that life knows what's happening.

There are many different forms of meditation, but at its core all meditation is the practice of taking a few minutes a day to stop and do absolutely nothing. No phone calls, e-mails, computers, talking, eating, television . . . nothing. Slow down the engine that runs your mind, and take time to focus on the engine that runs your body. When you simply acknowledge your breath—breathing in and out—you are tapping into your life force. Just allow everything to be exactly as it is. Sometimes, it feels good just to hang out in God's waiting room!

Isn't it extraordinary how much we fight the idea of being quiet? What are we afraid of? What's the worst that could happen? Who could come out and hurt us? What are we avoiding? There are few things more essential than taking five to ten minutes a day to find your center; it will help you handle anything going on in your life. *Just be quiet.* Nearly every religion encourages silence and solitude. Remember: whenever we lose something external during change, we always have the chance to regain an inner home.

My friend Maria found an answer she was looking for only when she took a few moments to get really quiet. After a blissful engagement, a three-day wedding celebration, and a monthlong honeymoon, she never imagined that marriage would be so difficult. But just one month into married life she had never been unhappier. She and her husband fought about money; about the time he spent with his friends, and about when to have a baby. They were once deeply in love, but now they felt like strangers. One night, after a particularly painful argument, Maria sat

> **No one ever feels vulnerable when they are aligned with who they are.**
> **—Esther Hicks**

alone on their bed after her husband stormed out. "I decided that the only solution was for me to leave. I picked a destination that was far, far away—Southeast Asia—and began to make a list of all the supplies I would need. And just as I was about to get up and research plane tickets, I caught the light of the moon through our bedroom window. As I stared into the night sky I got the sense that someone was listening. So I asked what I imagined was God or the universe if this man was right for me, if we could make it work. I remained quiet and still on the bed, and the answer came to me not in a big neon sign, but in a resounding peace that filled my body and mind. When my husband came home later that night, I saw him in a new light. I had let go of my expectations of what this marriage was supposed to be and had accepted it for what it was: flawed, but right for me. I knew something bigger was guiding me and always had been. I am grateful that I allowed myself to ask for help from something higher."

Prayer

Many of the people I have met who are going through change believe in prayer as a great tool. I don't usually ask whom they are praying to; that would be the wrong question. I simply ask whether it has helped them, and nearly everyone says yes. Prayer is simply another way to find a moment of connection to something we choose to believe in. This may be a person, an energy, or a loving presence. We can communicate through conversation, a cry for help, or a moment of thanks. We may turn to prayer as we surrender to an impossible situation or to remind ourselves that we are not in control and that a mystery much greater than us is at work. And sometimes, the best way to help someone else is to simply pray for him or her.

Recently, I spoke to a woman who used prayer to get through a series of terrifying changes. Christine was raped at the age of thirty while her daughter slept next to her. The man threatened to rape her child next if she said a word or fought back, and to kill them both if she called anyone within an hour after he left the house. Within a few months of that horror, while alone in the house, she was robbed by two armed men and left tied up in her living room. As if that weren't enough, she then found out her husband had had five affairs in their five years of marriage.

At this point Christine was incredibly mad at God and refused to pray or go to church. She wondered how a loving God could allow all these things to happen. But with time, she says, she saw that "blame wouldn't reverse any of this pain. I might never know the purpose of why I went through such hard times, but I knew that a life without prayer, or some feeling of closeness to God, would not make things any better. My first prayer was to have God take me home, to somehow be dead." But she then changed direction and prayed for inner peace and for the power to forgive her assailants. She even started praying for them as individuals. Eventually, her life regained some normalcy. "Prayer washed me clean again. It was my way of dealing, of getting all of that anger, hurt, and disbelief out in a safe way."

Prayer is very personal. You do it in your language, in your way. Whether it's a continuous open relationship with a known religious figure or something else you believe in, prayer can only help. There are no downsides. And prayer doesn't need to start when some big crisis occurs. Praying for just the day-to-day things is equally valuable and important.

The Big You Versus the Little You

The world is full of people who have stopped listening to the better part of themselves. It's maybe time for you to tune in to yourself again. You can start by examining the relationship between the Little You—the very human, ego-driven part of you, or your lower self—and the Big You—your higher self. Your lower self is often terrified, stuck, and longing for control, while your higher self reacts to change in a way that embraces and respects what is happening. It's like there's a relay race going on between the lower self and the higher self. Which part will determine how this change will be played out? It's a choice you make. The Little You wants to be right and take charge. The Big You wants to show you the way, make it simpler, and transport you to a happier, more peaceful place despite the obstacles you may face along the way.

You need to keep asking the Big You to make itself known, to take control, and to lead the journey instead of letting the mind (a.k.a. the Little You)—which is probably freaking out—take control. Get out of your own way. And if that seems difficult, take

> **Realize that there is a vast supply of universal power that you can tap into. This power doesn't come from us at all, yet we are all somehow connected to it. And we are either attracting it or keeping it away.**

comfort in knowing that there is at least one moment in the day—maybe right when you wake up—in which your mind hasn't had time to remind you of how terrible things are or how difficult this change is. That's when you are tapped into the real you, the Big You, your higher self.

When you practice higher-self behavior, you take the high road by not reacting quickly and instead choosing wisely how to respond. Activating your higher self puts you in tune with the best part of yourself, the part that turns to better thoughts and actions no matter what the circumstances are, no matter how hurt, angry, disappointed, or frustrated you may feel. Tuning in to this part of yourself will help you view your situation with clarity and make productive decisions with conviction.

Your lower self tends to slip into self-pity and hold grudges, saying things like *My life is nothing without this guy who just left me,* or *I can't forgive my parents for what they did when I was young,* or *My business is ruined now that this deal fell through,* or *I'm never going to be happy and healthy again.* Your higher self is the part of you that doesn't allow you to become a victim or to blame someone else or to get lost in anger. Your higher self helps you shine in your strength, compassion, and clarity. And your higher self gives a microphone to your heart and your soul, not only to your mind. One woman said it best when she admitted that she didn't realize she had it in her to be so courageous when her child died. She didn't think she would be able to access the source within her that supplies her with hope and strength. The more you seek out this part of yourself, the more you will receive from it.

Your primary responsibility during change is to be open to another part of you—not the overworked mind, but the underworked spirit and soul. Don't get me wrong: the mind is wonderful and we need it. But a little bit of mind and a little bit of soul is the right combination. Check in with yourself. How balanced are you in this equation? Most of us are a little too much of one and not enough of the other. But just by sparking the *intention* to believe in something bigger, you're already on your way to tapping into the higher part of yourself, and to becoming more conscious.

> *Your call to action is to act from your higher self. "What would the better, wiser, calmer part of me do or say or think right now?" That is the only question. It's what your intuition guides you to do—not the reactive, resistant side of you.*

How Can Your Spiritual Side Help During Change?

During the uncertain moments of change, your friends upstairs—God, or the Source—can be an invaluable resource. This force will help you use your inner compass, which guides you to what is best for you. And when you turn to your friends upstairs, you can ask them anything; there's no request too big or too small. You can ask for people to help you; you can ask to understand why something has happened; you can ask for a book recommendation, a choice parking spot, or financial support. The only trick is to actively believe that your request will be heard and answered. Sometimes you'll have to believe for days, weeks, or even months. And that's where so many of us fail. We give it a few days and then get disappointed when help hasn't arrived, instead of constantly renewing our faith and belief.

It's also important to start behaving as if what you have asked for is already in your life. Someone asked me the other day at a conference why I always seem to receive what I need. Without thinking, I replied, "I ask, and then I make space for it." It's important to become comfortable with the emptiness that needs to exist before the help arrives. Asking for guidance is step one, and creating the space and time for it to show up is step two.

✓ Take Action

1. Find moments when you have *not* trusted your intuition and higher self. What happened? (Personally, I started out by hiring the wrong people for my company, moved to the wrong city, went into business with the wrong firms, took jobs I didn't like, went out with the wrong guys, didn't make important decisions for fear of hurting someone else's feelings, and invested in the wrong stocks—all because I trusted my mind more than my heart and intuition!)

2. Recall a moment when you connected with your higher self. It may have been through prayer, meditation, a feeling of gratitude, or strong intuition about a person, a deal, or a decision. Did you receive a hunch or message about what to do?

3. If, just for a few moments, you chose to believe in your higher self or your friends upstairs, what would you ask of them? For at least the next thirty days, be willing to have a relationship with that part of you and to ask for help during this change.

4. Make a commitment to check in with your higher self at least once every day. Pick a time if it's easier. Ask for what you need, and be grateful for what you have. Start having a friendly conversation with this part of yourself. You are always communicating with yourself, but it's usually your mind that is doing all the talking without allowing your higher self to get a word in. Be open to how your higher self communicates: sometimes it's with words, and sometimes it's with a clever sign, suggestion, or funny coincidence that you come across during the day. Often it's a very strong hunch.

Trusting Your Intuition

Your higher self communicates through your intuition. We all know what feels right and what doesn't, and we know instinctively what is right and what is wrong. This ability is embedded in our DNA. We have just lost touch with that part of ourselves. We trust others more than ourselves, and in doing so we have weakened our internal sense of guidance and judgment. Now is the time to check back in with your higher self and use the gift of intuition that we have all been given.

Your intuition and your higher self work together; one cannot function without the other. During times of change, listen closely to that part of you that knows, the part that keeps nudging you in the right direction, however uncomfortable the message.

We tend to get into the pattern of ignoring our intuition because, too often, acknowledging your intuition may involve making a difficult decision, perhaps leaving a job you know is wrong for you or a relationship that makes you unhappy, or realizing that you are slowly killing yourself from an addiction. Whatever it is, your intuition will always tell you the truth about a situation. We hope that if we ignore our intuition, the problem will go away. We don't want to do the inner work of healing, grieving, or facing the consequences of our actions. We ignore our intuition because we are convinced we know better, that what we *think*—as opposed to what we *feel*—is always right. Though our intuition is always powered on and ready to help us, most of the time it's not something we give a microphone to. Our mind's microphone is much louder. It

> *My friend Patrick says: "Most people have two pets they take care of—the mind and the body. And most people spend all their time focusing on the mind, where the ego lives, and no time on the body, where intuition and gut feelings live."*

seems easier to place our trust in our mind, intellect, and actions than in this intangible thing called intuition.

One way to tap into your intuition is by listening to your body. Your intuition is that part of you that makes your stomach tight if something is off, gives you a headache when something isn't right, or makes you breathe quicker if it wants you to take note of something. Your intuition doesn't allow you to sleep at night if you are making a wrong decision, and it can cause you to eat aimlessly if you are ignoring a sign that you are not moving in the right direction. Intuition is what lets you know whether a person, a job, a decision, or a deal isn't right for you; it wakes you up in the morning, trying to get your attention about something before your mind has fully awakened; or it makes you not want to go to work when you know it's wrong. Intuition repeats thoughts, ideas, feelings, and concerns until you finally listen.

When we don't listen to our intuition, the results can be disastrous. The mother of a dear friend of mine learned this firsthand. Her doctor recommended surgery to remove a small abnormality in her uterus. For months she delayed the procedure. Something kept telling her this was a bad idea, that the doctor was being overly aggressive in his approach, and that there would be complications after her surgery. She ultimately decided to go against her intuition and follow the doctor's medical advice, which her family also supported. The surgery nearly killed her. The surgeon accidentally cut into her small intestine, putting her into a coma for a few days. She spent two months in intensive care, and the whole ordeal lasted close to four months.

This woman's story doesn't mean you should disregard the advice of your doctor or any other "expert" in your life. It's simply a reminder to heed the red flags that your intuition may present. There is always more than one way to look at a situation, and your intuition may guide you to the option that is in your best interest.

Tune Your Antennae

Another way to tap into your spiritual side is to become more open to the language of life, as I mentioned earlier. We all receive signs and directions, but we don't know where they come from. They take all forms, shapes, and sizes: a book you hear about, a phone call from a friend suggesting something, an article you read in the newspaper that describes exactly what you are going through, a chance meeting with someone, a class or event you happen to hear about.

Don't let your mind rationalize away these external signs. Take them for what they are, and then decide whether they are there to guide you. If you believe in them, they will show up even more, like signposts along an uncertain path, giving you directions. You don't have to follow these signs; just be open to seeing them. I constantly use the analogy of having antennae on my head. On a daily basis, I am tuning in to all the ways that life and my intuition may be trying to help me through change. I say to myself, *I am in perfect synchronicity with life.*

When Diane fine-tuned her antennae, she could hardly believe the miracle it brought to her life. She and her husband had been trying to have kids for five years. Each miscarriage was a crushing blow to them and their marriage. They had seen every fertility specialist in their city and had even begun alternative treatments, but with no luck. Their marriage was beginning to fall apart. Then, one day, while she was up late watching TV with her husband, a news report came on about adoption in China. They were tuned to a channel they rarely watched, but for some reason they chose it that night. The news report told of how so many Chinese orphans needed homes. Normally, they might have looked at this as a sad story but one that did not have anything to do with them. But Diane saw it as a sign. Why were they up at this hour watching TV? Why this channel? Why this news report? They soon began to inquire about adoption, and within two years they were the proud parents of a baby girl.

Take Responsibility

Often, we look for people to guide us. On the outside, these people may appear better than we are, more educated or knowledgeable, with more charisma and power. We may look for a father type to make us feel more certain and safe, or a mother type to make us feel loved and accepted. But one of the big mistakes we make is to abdicate responsibility to someone else: we are quick to give our trust to someone in a position of authority and become a follower. Although friends, family members, doctors, and therapists all have tremendous value, no one else can really get in touch with our own intuition or the lesson we need to learn. That journey is one we must take alone.

Do not sacrifice your own intuition or your own intelligence; do not give that space over exclusively to a specialist, to someone who seems to know more than you—a mentor, a guru, or even a set of friends. Incorporate the best of what you hear and learn, but always come back to yourself. You have wisdom inside. In India, they chant the words *"wa he guru,"* which honors the guru within and is said to remove all obstacles. You are much, much more intuitive than you have ever been told. Intuition is not some special power only *other* people have. Perhaps this little prayer will help you align yourself to your intuition. When I am in the midst of a change, when I fear making a wrong decision, or when things seem not to be working, I say the following:

Now you got my attention.
I am not running anymore.
What's next?
Show me the way.

I also constantly speak to my friends upstairs—making requests, thanking them, and posing questions about things I don't understand. I also get mad at them. I sulk, get pissed off, and resent them for things that have or have not happened in my life. Sometimes I ignore them—and they laugh. When I am lonely, I immediately ask them to surround me. They are part of my team—all-knowing, all-loving protectors that are always there.

No, I have never met them. I don't know what they look like or how many of them there are. But when I need something, I ask them for it. And do you know what? It's amazing how often I feel their guidance and assistance. Some of us don't know or believe that our "friends upstairs" exist, so we certainly don't give them any work to do. They're unemployed! I joke sometimes that I have an "Ariane to-do list" for things I can accomplish and a "Universe to-do list" for things that I can't do alone. And after I make the second list I don't check to see whether every item has been addressed; I wait patiently, understanding that help is on the way. When and how help will arrive is a mystery, and I welcome the chance to let it unfold as it will.

Again, it doesn't matter how you label the higher sources you access or what exactly you believe them to be. I don't know if these friends of mine are an energy inside of me or are actually "upstairs"; what matters is that your belief in them activates a part of you that is unchanging, one that is much more powerful than the Little You who gets scared and insecure. I prefer imagining that they have access to great people, ideas, and solutions—and are capable of great miracles. I ask them for help with just about anything—business decisions, financial matters, hassle-free travel, or personal problems I may be facing. But I do my bit as well. This isn't passive delegation; it's active participation. I actively believe that I am not alone, and I work to get into the flow of life. I remember to go *with* the river and not to resist it, and to take action where necessary. And I am always open to what my inner guidance is telling me. Sometimes I wonder why I didn't ask for more help in the past. But I've learned that it takes practice to step aside and let something else assist in any situation of change, whether it's at a job interview or at the doctor's office. Whenever I am off center, I nearly always find that I am acting from a place of ego, of mind, or of control. I see that I haven't checked in with the other side of myself, my spiritual side. The first thirty days of any change are a great time to get comfortable with this other part of you, the connection you have to your soul, to something of your own that is simply wiser.

What is right for me won't be right for someone else. But if you'd like to embrace your spiritual side and are unsure about how, just know that something always feels either good or bad. When you can sense the difference between the two, you are in tune with your spirit. And connecting to this part of us isn't necessarily linked to religion, or to anything New Age; it's something that's always inside of us. So when you say, "I don't know what to do," you need to tap into your inner guidance system. Often you do know what to do; you just don't want to acknowledge it if moving in that direction requires work—which it usually does! When you reach for an action or thought that makes you feel better, you are aligning with your spiritual side. The more you tune in to your higher self and intuition, the better you'll get at knowing yourself, reading yourself, and seeing how something feels.

✓ Take Action

Practice tuning in to your intuition for thirty days. How? Concentrate on how you *feel* about something instead of what you *think* about something. Simply train yourself to ask: *How does this feel? Good, or not so good?* Intuition always gives you a choice.

The first thirty days of any change are the ideal time to begin getting in touch with your spiritual side. It's during these first few days and weeks of change that you truly need to be grounded, to know without a shadow of a doubt that things will be OK, that things will work out, that you will make it through. During your stuck states—those moments when your head hurts because your mind can't figure it out—life invites you to awaken another part of yourself: the higher part. Instead of gracefully activating the inner guidance we have inside, we are conditioned to struggle, to stress, and to create minidramas. When we're struggling, trusting our inner guides and turning to prayer and meditation may not seem so useful, especially if they don't yield immediate answers and results. But if we can allow everything to be as it is—even if it's just for a couple of hours, or days—if we can be patient and accept our current reality, we can begin the inner work, the inquiry into the change. We can ask our friends upstairs what the next best steps should be.

> *People can't live with change if there is not a changeless core inside them.*
> *—Stephen R. Covey*

The spiritual road is often outside most of our comfort zones, and it may feel too New Agey, but it works—not only for me, but for millions of other people who have found it possible to bring a sense of grace to any situation. We are in a state of grace when we give up the struggle for a while and allow something else to take over. I believe that all of us—nature, animals, human beings—are connected to something higher. We need to ask ourselves why we have forgotten this connection.

All I suggest is for you to start the conversation with yourself. Go inside, ask for help, listen to your intuition, look for signs, pray or meditate. And don't forget to have gratitude, to say thank you when you do feel guided, when you do get an answer, when something you wanted does come through. As you become more and more grateful for what you have been given, the spiritual side of you becomes more active in your life, taking even better care of you during change. So, while my first thought in the morning is to offer up an intention for the day, in the evening my final thoughts, regardless of how difficult my day was, are always about gratitude. I even have a gratitude journal in which I focus on what was great about that day. Try it and see how much better you feel.

God is preparing you for greater things. He's going to take you further than you thought possible, so don't be surprised when He asks you to think better of yourself and to act accordingly.
—Joel Osteen

The first thirty days are the time to take the first steps in the right direction—inside yourself. Your higher self and your connection to something bigger will be there to carry you through this journey of change.

The First 30 Days: What to Remember

1. You are connected to something bigger that can help and guide you. Reconnect with your spirit, your soul, and your higher self, and the journey through change will be calmer.

2. Many of the answers and advice you're looking for are already inside of you. Trust yourself and your intuition to guide you.

3. There are many ways to be aligned with your spiritual side: prayer, mediation, silence, nature, church. . . . Find the way that feels right for you.

> *Now is the time for guts and God.*
> *—Elizabeth Taylor*

Your Change Support Team

The People and Things That Can Help

Principle 8: People who successfully navigate change are not alone; they surround themselves with people who can help, who have the right beliefs and skills. And they create an environment that supports their change.

One of our biggest flaws as human beings is that we keep thinking we are alone. Whatever the situation, there is always, always someone who can help.

In moments of transition, it's normal to feel alone. We convince ourselves that our situation is unique—that no one has gone through this specific change before, or all these changes at once. We think the changes we face are so distinct that no one else can help or understand us. So what do we do? We isolate ourselves, retreating into an inner world of pity and stress. All signs tell us that this is going to be a long journey to loneliness.

Saying three simple words—*I need help*—opens up channels of assistance. Most of us think that saying those words makes us weak. We worry about what someone might think or say if we admit we don't have it all figured out. We are not meant to isolate ourselves during change. We are meant to stay connected, to relate to others, to be around people who have an optimistic mind-set, and to offer and receive help and support. We all feel better after we have offered assistance to another person. Think back to the last few times a friend reached out to you for help. He or she may have been going through a breakup, illness, infidelity, or problems with a child. Remember how rewarding it was to know you could be there for someone else? Give someone the gift of being able to help you out of hiding, out of a place where you are suffering unnecessarily.

My friend Kathy is one of the best examples of understanding how to move through change. Her life started out with complications during her birth, and change has been challenging her ever since. Growing up, she was molested in her own home and was so unhappy that she tried to commit suicide five times. Later she would survive being run over by a Jeep and struggling with two bouts of cancer only to go on to become the first hearing-impaired comedian. When it comes to change, Kathy knows all about it.

"It's essential to be grateful," she says. "I never asked 'Why?' because I realized those three letters had no answers. But people really helped me through every one of the changes I was given. The only real way out of change is to let someone know you're stuck. There are always people around to help you, but you have to make the choice to seek them out. That is your responsibility alone."

There are many reasons why we hide: We don't want to damage the perception other people have of us. We feel ashamed to admit that we don't know the answer and that we are afraid and unsure. We may be hesitant to bother our friends with our problems, or we don't think anyone else has been through what we're going through. But it is our ego that often stops us from asking for help. We believe we should be able to get ourselves out of the hole without help from anyone else.

Sometimes opening up to those who have proven expertise can be the perfect compromise. Your friends care about you, but they don't have the specific knowledge that can help you through the change. You can reach out to your pastor or a marriage counselor, you can go online to find people who are going through similar changes, or you can start seeing a therapist. Remember, you are not supposed to know everything. You are not meant to know how to deal with a parent who has had a stroke or to cope with the loss of a child. There is so much help out there. If you find it hard to ask for help or a favor, commit to asking for three small things a day from people. Take the initial discomfort out, and see how easy it becomes when you let people in.

Your Team

People have an easier time with change when they surround themselves with other people. These other people allow them to change, even to embrace their changes, while creating a very positive environment that supports what they are going through. Change is always easier when we let other people in, when we share the change, the struggle, or when we ask for encouragement or advice. One of the quickest ways to embrace change is to surround yourself with a team of people. Your team can be made up of any number of people from any area of your life—family, friends, colleagues, clergy members, teachers, and so on—as long as they each support, inspire, and motivate you in some way.

I have chosen a very specific team to surround me. During times of change, I remember that these people are always there; they never disappear.

My team . . .

. . . won't allow me to stay stuck for very long. They will kindly kick me in the butt when I feel I can't go on.

. . . are optimists who believe in me and in life. They encourage and motivate me.

. . . at least one person has been through the change I need help with.

. . . give me the perspective of different backgrounds, ideas, and professions. They continually teach me things, keeping me open-minded. Their uniqueness helps me see things from different angles.

. . . is made up of people who each have a specific area of strength (humor, planning, health) that I respect and can learn from.

. . . give me a safe place to land if I need to share or express a thought or emotion.

My team was not always this healthy. I used to spend a lot of time with people just like me—people who didn't like their jobs, who couldn't find time to exercise, who complained about their friends and family, and who had stories about why their lives weren't what they wanted them to be. These people were safe and comfortable. When I was around them I never needed to step up and I never needed to change my thoughts or behavior. I saw that some of these people wanted me to stay stuck, to not have my business take off and I began to understand that some people are givers while others are takers.

Did I just chuck these people out of my life? No, but I made a conscious choice to reach out to other people who I knew would push me and help me grow. When actively trying to change an aspect of your life, change the people you spend the most time with. You may find yourself thinking: *Oh, they're nice people. They can't be holding me back or making change harder.* But you'll find that you mirror their beliefs, behaviors, values, language, and actions —or lack of actions—so be very mindful about the company you keep. Sometimes the person you spend the most time with may be the one holding you back from a change. If you want to really change your life, look at the four or five people you spend the most time with. They exert a huge influence on your life.

I experienced the power of my team when I focused on two goals I had: keeping fit and becoming financially confident. I surrounded myself with people who are living the way I aspire to live. Some work out every day! Others have made millions! By simply spending time with these people, I learn and am inspired to reach and maintain a certain standard. Sometimes it's uncomfortable to spend time with people who have something you want, but the discomfort means that you are growing and that you will reach their level quicker. If you hang around the action, soon enough you will become part of it.

☑ Take Action

1. Who is on your team today?

2. In what ways are they a positive influence? In what ways might they hold you back?

3. What do you want to change in your life? Is someone on your team able to help you fulfill this change?

4. If you want to change your health, do you have healthy people on your team? If you want to be married, do you have a married couple on your team? If you want to be wealthy, do you have someone with strong financial know-how on your team? You must surround yourself with people who have already success-fully made or faced the change you are in.

5. When you are actively trying to change an aspect of your life, change the people you spend the most time with. Who doesn't need to be on your go-to team anymore? Would your relation-ship with him or her be healthier if he or she had less influence on your life?

6. Who *should* be on your team today? Reach out to them.

I remember that when I started an MBA program at Stanford, I felt like a fish out of water. I grew up in Asia, went to school in England, and had never worked or lived in the United States. My accent was different, my method of studying and speaking up in class was different, and I was the youngest in the class by far—just twenty-two. And my back-ground wasn't in hard-core finance or business, so on top of all that, it seemed like I was significantly behind all the time. I felt very alone, but my insecurities kept me from asking for help and from seeking out others. Then I reconnected with an old friend, Joe, who

> *Every one of us gets through the tough times because somebody is there, standing in the gap to close it for us.*
> —*Oprah Winfrey*

called me religiously once a day to check in. During those calls, I could be honest with him—freaking out before exams or at the mountain of work I was facing. It may have helped that this friend wasn't in school with me: sometimes the best help comes from a person who *isn't* sitting right next to you. He was a constant source of encouragement and always helped to restore my belief in my abilities. I'm not sure I could have made it without him.

Slowly, over time, I admitted to my parents, to some friends, and even to some of my classmates that all was not well in Ariane's world. In a matter of weeks, I had a team of supporters who would not let me fail. They called, sent encouraging cards and gifts, and tried to help in any other way they could. I even had a few people come visit. As things got better, I realized that other classmates were just as lost and overwhelmed as I was. I was not alone. I soon found my footing and started enjoying myself.

Ask yourself who has been there for you in the past when you were going through a big change. Who checked in, and who kept you going? If you haven't done so, take a moment to call them, write them a note, acknowledge them.

Honesty and Specificity

You can receive help only if you are honest about what you need. Often, simply telling someone you need help isn't enough. For example, a friend of mine recently made it clear that she wants to change careers. She has been telling me how unhappy she is at her job for over a year, but I'm still not sure how I can really help her. Does she want advice? Does she want me to kick her in the butt so she takes some action? Does she want me to help her create a plan? Remember, people all around you want to help.

They really do. But if you want to be able to benefit from their help, be clear about what it is you need from them.

Do you need someone to call you, to come around and check in on you? Do you need someone to help you move? Do you need someone to help with your finances? Do you need help changing your diet? Do you need help cleaning out your closets? Do you need help getting a makeover? Help using your computer? Help understanding how to work the machines in the gym? Help changing your negative outlook or letting go of something you are still stuck on from the past?

It's natural to be vague when we're with our friends or support network. After all, just the act of asking for help is hard enough. When we do get the courage to reach out, voicing our specific needs feels even more challenging. Instead, we often turn to our team to forget about something or just to vent. But our time would be so much more effective if we also said: *I really need your help. Can you do this for me? Recommend a book or a coach?* And then stand back and watch the support roll in.

Staying in the Hole or Climbing Up the Ladder

Are you choosing to stay in the hole or to climb up the ladder? Your answer to this question will influence who is on your team. When seeking help during change, it's important to distinguish between two types of people: those who get in the hole with you and stay there, and those who see you in the hole, throw you a ladder, and coach you up the ladder. If you want to remain a victim, you often gravitate toward friends who keep you stuck. If you are determined to move forward and leave behind a place of insecurity and suffering, turn to those who will motivate you.

Which of your friends will always help you climb up the ladder? These people may frustrate you sometimes because you'd like them to feel sorry for you; but they will never get in the hole and be miserable with you. These are great friends.

After a divorce and a series of emotionally empty relationships, Joan received the best form of support from her oldest friend, a key member of her team. After Joan had fallen for yet another man who did not reciprocate her affection, Joan's friend told her—in no uncertain terms—that she has a constant, unconscious attraction to men who are emotionally unavailable—specifically, men who aren't kind and giving. This astute observation completely knocked Joan over, but the empowering—and, yes, very painful—life lesson forced her to examine those in her past, a virtual lineup of the emotionally unavailable. She realized that the pattern began with her father and mother and moved on to her ex-husband and most of the guys she had dated. "Until my friend spoke up, I was completely and utterly clueless that this was a forty-five-year-old pattern," Joan says. "I am forever blessed by her insight and the newfound wisdom of knowing I can—and am—breaking destructive patterns that have run my life for years."

Joan's friend was an RSH—a Real Source of Help—someone who

- puts you back in control and shows you your choices while you are in the midst of change;

- asks you the right questions and doesn't tell you what to do;

- presents you with options, information, and inspiration but ultimately makes it clear that you are in the driver's seat;

- helps you get unstuck and gives you a new perspective while giving you a safe space to explore what's really going on.

An RSH is someone you respect, someone who is wise and who often has had experience with a similar change and can help you through yours.

There's an old story I love that shows the power of a real source of help. An Indian woman and her son traveled thousands of miles by train to meet Mahatma Gandhi. Her son was addicted to sugar, and she was getting concerned about his health. Since Gandhi was the man her son most respected, she thought, *If he can tell him to stop eating sugar, then my son will surely stop.* After many days of traveling and hours of waiting in line, the woman approached Gandhi and asked him for his help. Gandhi looked at the boy and then told his mother to come back in a few weeks. She was discouraged but nevertheless agreed. She began the journey all over again, and when she came before Gandhi the second time, all he said to her son was, "Stop eating sugar." And the boy was healed. Now the mother was slightly annoyed and asked, "Sir, with all respect, why couldn't you tell him that a month ago when we first met you?" Gandhi replied, "Because a month ago, *I* was still eating sugar."

> *Only to the extent that we expose ourselves over and over again to annihilation can that which is indestructible arise within us. In this lies the dignity of daring.*
> *—Karlfried Dürckheim*

So you see, an RSH has integrity. Real sources of help match their actions to their words, will be honest, and have often gone through a similar change. And if they can't help, they will say so.

When seeking out real sources of help, find people whom you relate to. If you have lost someone you love, find people you like and trust who have gone through something similar. If you are going through infertility issues, find others who have had to make similar choices. If you have a troubled teenager, seek out others who have gone through the same thing. They may have some perspective on what helped and can share the mistakes they made and what they learned. Your intuition knows who can help you. Look deep inside and ask yourself: *Who can really help me with what I am going through right now? Who has good, healthy self-esteem? Who is happy in their life?* Use your power of discernment to discover who can serve you best.

Expanding Your Social Circle: Your Team Is Not Always Who You Think!

Be open to new people and resources coming into your life. Change is a cycle of death and rebirth: old events and relationships will fall away as new ones appear. Don't rely on what has always been there to help you for what you are going through today. Sometimes a brand-new acquaintance who knows nothing about you, who sees you for who you are today and not yesterday, can be the answer. With someone new, we may be more willing to be honest and authentic about who we are and what we are going through, without trying desperately to preserve the image of who we once were. Look beyond the familiar for help. It may come in ways you never imagined.

Ashley received an incredible amount of help from an unexpected team when she experienced a great tragedy. She was twenty-five years old and just weeks away from getting married when she and her fiancé went down to city hall to pick up their marriage certificate. "We'd been engaged around ten months. It was the most exciting time in my life. I was ready to get married,

I had my dress, and we had the place. Everything was ready to go. Our honeymoon was even booked," Ashley says. And then everything changed when, along the way, her fiancé suddenly became dizzy and nauseous, and stepped between two subway cars for some air. He passed out, fell into the space between the cars, and was killed instantly on the tracks.

The one thing that really made all the difference for Ashley in the days and months that followed the accident was connecting with three people who had all lived through similar situations. "Those three people were what got me through. The two women were especially inspiring because one had since gotten married and was pregnant at the time. And I thought, *Wow, look where life has taken her since the accident.* And the other one had moved onto a new relationship. I still keep in touch with both women, because they really showed me that there was a future ahead for me, that it was possible to be happy again."

The third person in Ashley's support group—a man who had lost his fiancée a couple of months earlier to an illness—handled his grief in a dramatically different manner but was equally helpful to her healing. "I always thought, 'I have to get up, I have to take a shower, I have to get dressed.' I believed that if I didn't do it one day, I would get stuck. But this guy was wallowing in grief. He couldn't get up in the morning. And I felt like I was able to give him advice, which really helped me," Ashley says. Guiding another person through a serious time of grief motivated Ashley to move through her own pain and suffering. "I just knew I had to get through the next day and the day after that. And then it was getting through the next week. And then it was getting through the first month."

Sometimes life will ask you to be an example for someone else. It may be someone you know who counts on you for your resilience, strength, and powerful change muscle. These people are also on your team. Without knowing it, they are asking you to be a hero of some sort, and in doing so they will help you move through change quicker.

Comparison Sickness

When change beckons, we also have a tendency to compare our situation to that of others: *Why is their life so much better than mine? Why do things appear easier for them? If only I were in their shoes, things would be so much easier. If I had their money or youth, this change would be easier.* We compare everything: social status, relationship status, looks, jobs, financial standing, success in the world, friends and lovers, kids, homes, and luck.

Many times we don't reach for help because we are ashamed, because we have been busy comparing our problems with someone else's problem. We compare ourselves with others who seem to have it all together. Or we minimize our problem vis-à-vis the problems of the world, asking, *How can I seek out help with this little problem when so many people are poor, starving, or sick?*

Here is a great story about comparisons and complaints. One day, God was listening to all the comparisons people were making to others, and he asked each person to put all their problems in a transparent bag and place it in a separate room. Then he asked everyone to line up and, one by one, go into this room and pick a bag, any bag. Since the bags were transparent, everyone could see what others were going through—all of the changes in their lives, the decisions they had to make, their complaints, and their struggles with others. The first person looked around at all the bags and finally decided to leave with his own bag. The next person did the same thing: she left with the bag she dropped off. In the end, everyone picked his or her own bag. Why? Because we are meant to work through our own problems, changes, and crises. Even though it may not feel like it in the moment, you have not been given anything that you cannot handle. In fact, you're an expert in dealing with your unique set of challenges.

After living in Los Angeles as a single woman for over twelve years, Jenny was tired of being alone and blamed herself for not finding a partner. Beat down by comparison sickness, she isolated herself from all of her married friends and even the friends who were dating. "Every day it seems that more beautiful, skinny, perfect women descend upon this town—and every day I don't seem to be getting any younger or skinnier," she says. " I used to spend nights at home, watching television or doing some other mindless work to avoid the inevitable comparison. But recently, I started wearing a bracelet that reminded me to just be myself. I can't change my background or my looks or my age, and I am sick of comparing myself. I realized that you can't control love. When it's your time, it's your time. Exactly a year after I made that declaration to myself, I got engaged to a wonderful man."

Comparison sickness is an epidemic that we all suffer from in varying degrees. Take a moment to remember what you have to offer, your unique talents, what makes you *you*. Then face this change with everything you've got, not with what anyone else may or may not have.

Creating the Ultimate Change Environment

People are essential during times of change, but so are the spaces in which you live and work and the things you choose to surround yourself with. When going through change, surround yourself with things that are symbols of comfort, positive memories, or power so that if you lose your way, they're there as a compass to get you back on course. It can be a teddy bear, a trinket, a note someone wrote to you, a card, a candle, a photo of something or someone, a journal, some inspirational quotes tacked up on the wall, or a lucky stone. There are no rules or limitations for the things that give you strength.

I have lots of reminders that help me through life, like the quote on my screen saver: "From this situation, only good will come." I also have a few lucky stones I carry in my bag; some I chose, and some were given me. I usually have a candle burning when I am at home. For me, a candle always brings light to any situation: all the darkness in the world cannot put out the light of one candle. I also have specific things that I surround myself with during times of intense change: music that helps me feel grounded; a lucky phrase on my cell phone; the journal I've been writing in for five years; photos of friends and people I love; sage and incense that I burn to cleanse a space and bring in the new; and a lucky bracelet (engraved with "Stay true to who you are").

I'm not the only one who uses symbols and reminders to get through change.

Joe has a little statue of Buddha. "It reminds me of how everything is always changing, not to cling to anything as permanent, to welcome change, and to sit through the uncomfortableness," he says.

Andrew has a laminated change affirmation card with five things that he wants to continually remember, like *Everything happens for a reason and a purpose that serves me.*

Edward has a small felt bag containing a couple of lucky stones that he picked up from a few places around the world and a piece of string that represents his ability to always find his way through change.

Christine has a small crucifix. "Jesus represents the ultimate change for me, going from dying on a cross to resurrecting," she says.

Pete carries photos of his kids. "I always think about how much they have changed and continue to change. It's an immediate reminder that change can be a good thing," he says.

What symbol might help you during times of change? For me, it's also always been blue envelopes. Yes, blue envelopes. When I was twelve years old and at boarding school in England, desperately unhappy, lonely, unpopular, and living in a bathroom that had been converted into a bedroom, my mother, who lived thousands of miles away, would write to me every other day. She sent her notes in blue airmail envelopes, and those letters and that shade of blue became symbols for getting through really tough times. They were my lifeline. Today, whenever I think of those letters, even when I connect to the color blue, I feel the strength they gave me to keep going. My company now uses blue envelopes.

It's time to surround yourself with the things that help you feel strong, centered, and empowered.

Changing Your Environment

You also have permission to change your environment if it's not serving you during a time of change. Even if it's just for a day or half a day, a new place will give you a new perspective. Use the first thirty days of change to experiment with mixing up your routine: take a much-needed vacation for a week or two; go to the beach for the day; or take some time away from your parents or kids. It can be as simple as working in a café if you usually work at home, or taking a long walk in the park after work instead of rushing home.

The Power of a New Environment

I met a teenager who desperately wanted to come out of the closet. When he told his parents he was gay, life at home became extremely difficult for all of them. Eventually, he decided that he needed his own apartment. In a matter of months, the relationship with his parents dramatically improved and the young man started living in accordance with his new identity.

Sometimes the place where we live keeps us stuck. When I returned to Brussels for my last two years of high school, things at home were very difficult. Going from the structure and rules of boarding school back to a tense home environment with my parents didn't help me with my studies or with my overall happiness. So I spoke to my godfather, who had a small, empty apartment close by, and I eventually moved in there. I was fifteen, and although it was a bit terrifying to be living alone, it was by far the better option for me. My relationship with my dad improved, my grades skyrocketed, and I learned to be fully independent early on (and as a bonus, my godfather became a dependable member of my team for the next two years).

Our lives are full of things that can help us get through change; we just need to open our eyes to see them. And once we do, we need to find the courage to make some necessary shifts in our environment and in our team, whether small or drastic. But be aware: as you look to surround yourself with people and things that can help, your inner victim will make itself known. It's the part of you that wants you to believe you are alone, that no one else can help, that no one will understand, and that a change in your environment isn't necessary. When my inner victim recently came out, I made a huge effort to say: *No, go away. I don't need you. I will not choose to believe what you are feeding me.*

You are in charge now.

If you were to ask, *What is the truth?* you would find that the truth says there are always people and things that can help—in every situation you can imagine.

The First 30 Days: What to Remember

1. You are never alone. There is always someone who can help.

2. Change is easier and quicker when you reach out to others and have a strong positive team around you.

3. Rearrange your environment to support you, and find at least one symbol or object that will give you optimism and help you move through change.

Get Unstuck

*Actions to Move You Through
Any Change*

Principle 9: People who successfully navigate change take action. They have a plan and know how to take care of themselves.

Actions come in many forms. Some are big and obvious; some are so small you may think they are irrelevant. But any good action you take is a choice to move forward.

During the first thirty days of any change, the voice that says *I don't know what to do* becomes louder than usual. We become stuck. Scared of making the wrong decision, we don't act, and our negative emotions—change demons—keep telling us there doesn't seem to be an easy way to start.

But it is during this time of change that we most need to take action. People who keep moving forward take care of themselves. They have a plan and know what they want. Even a small effort helps you have an easier time moving through change.

Several years ago I was faced with the type of change you pray never enters your life—the death of a dear friend. Albert was the kind of friend everyone should be lucky enough to have. A larger-than-life, unconditionally loving man, he was always kind, always making people laugh, and always thinking of others before himself. I never imagined life without him.

When I got the call that he had been killed in a motorbike accident in Thailand, I was stunned. I was working in New York at the time and found that being so far away made the situation even more unreal. The days that followed were horrible. I didn't have anyone to share my feelings with: nobody in New York knew Albert. Alone, I cried and prayed and tried to remember some of the funny times we shared. He laughed at everything, and he'd have wanted me laughing as well.

> **The journey of a thousand miles begins with a step.**
> **—Lao-tzu**

I also got myself to the gym. Albert had been on a mission to lose weight, and I decided that one way to honor him and his passing would be to go to the gym myself. (I didn't know at the time about how exercise is a saving grace for anyone going through change.) Eventually it became a habit. I associated going to the gym and getting fit with our friendship, as if we were sharing a mutual goal and desire. Sooner than I imagined possible, I felt lighter, I could breathe again, and I wasn't staying home being miserable.

The actions I took following his passing were all things I knew he would have wanted me to do: get in fabulous shape, launch my business, laugh at everything possible, and remember that he wasn't too far away. The grieving passed, and the actions remained. I still do all the things that helped at the time, so Albert is ever present in my life today.

The Seed of New Beginnings

Yes, change takes work and change takes time. There are no shortcuts. Establishing discipline in your life—even for the small tasks—is a path to freedom, because it puts you in the driver's seat. You are not a victim of the whims and winds of change; you are *steering the boat.*

During any transition people always say the same thing: it's essential to take care of yourself during change. Even if it's actually the hardest thing to do, taking care of yourself is a non-optional part of moving through change. And when you take care of yourself, you'll see that your well-being is something you can actually control.

> *Inaction breeds doubt and fear. Action breeds confidence and courage. If you want to conquer fear, do not sit home and think about it. Go out and get busy.*
> **—Dale Carnegie**

Begin with the foundational *SEED of change,* as I call it: Sleep, Eat, Exercise, Drink (water, that is!).

You may look at this and think, *Oh, I'm doing all of those things already.* But I'll bet you aren't doing them nearly as often as you could be, or that you could be doing them in a healthier way. During change it's easy not to sleep enough or to stay in bed too much. You may also find yourself eating to avoid facing your change demons or not eating because you can't seem to drag yourself to the grocery story. And exercise may seem too time-consuming or difficult. When it comes to drinking, you may find that you keep yourself going with soda, coffee, and alcohol when water would serve you best. Whatever the change is—if your child has been diagnosed with ADD, or your parent has Alzheimer's, or you're starting a new business—without the proper foundation in your life, the SEED of change, you won't be able to handle the change well.

How to Take Action When You're Feeling Stuck

When stressful or overwhelming situations arise, it's tempting to curl up in a ball and hide—even if they're good changes. But any bit of movement you make will actually help dissipate the tension and anxiety you're feeling and will get you through the darkness and into a new phase of light. There is no perfect solution to moving through change, but taking action—even baby steps— can have a powerful effect on your life. In the following section you'll find some steps that will help you move through any change. Keep them visible somewhere. If you follow them, they can have a huge impact during the first thirty days and beyond.

1. Focus on Your Health

Change takes a lot of energy. So be mindful of replenishing your body or you will find yourself running on empty. Even doing something as basic as maintaining a healthy physical condition will make a world of difference. If you are feeling healthy, strong, fit, sexy, and happy with your body on a regular basis, you will have a healthy foundation of energy and self-esteem. But what do we do? Instead of turning to our health to make us feel better, we abandon it. In fact, when we are going through a change, it is often one of the first areas we let go; we get lethargic and become irresponsible about our fitness and diet.

Give your body a break. It's on your side and wants you back on your feet. Increase your physical exercise, and spend time being good to yourself with massages, walks, healthy foods, and vitamins. Flip your priorities: the next time you experience a big change, put exercise and doing good things for your health and body first, ahead of anything else.

Remember, you cannot stay in an emotionally stuck place when you are using your body. Different emotions are accessed when you exercise, emotions that make you feel better and boost your confidence. Also, we release psychic and mental energy through the body when we move. Yoga, walking, and biking are all wonderful ways of letting this energy out and preventing us from feeling heavy, tired, and sluggish.

Movement is essential during transitions because it prevents us from getting stuck. When we are going through change, we need to physically move because lots of energy is swirling around within us—emotional, physical, and psychic energy. When we stay still, or stuck, that energy is not circulating. So when you hear yourself say, "I don't know what to do," start moving. Exercise, clean the house, go grocery shopping—just get up and go anywhere. That's always the right answer!

The ex-wife of a friend of mine was forty-two when she began to bike, run, and swim. She started working out during her separation from her husband, and within a year their divorce was final and she was competing in triathlons. Three years later she now has sponsors and is the top performer in her age group. As she says, she lost a husband but gained a dream, a fabulous body, and tons of self-esteem. Taking care of your health can start at any age and is a huge factor in helping you move through change.

2. Turn to the Familiar

We too often assume that because a big change is happening, *everything* has changed. But plenty of things are still the same; our normal routine still exists. Doing the small, mundane things helps reassure us. Maybe you always go for a walk in the evenings, go to a certain coffee shop on Saturday, or go to church on Sunday. Taking small steps in a familiar direction will build your level of self-esteem and will re-engage your change muscle. The action, regardless of how small, creates a sense of result and movement. There's a tiny sense of victory and completion in every act.

> *No action, no change. Limited action, limited change. Lots of action, change occurs.*
> *—Catherine Pulsifer*

3. Take Care of the Little Things

Removing clutter builds confidence during change because it puts you in control of your life. It's critical to stay organized and not let little things pile up. This may mean anything from rearranging the furniture to paying your bills. Soon you will feel the power of choice returning rather than the uncertainty of the future dictating your life.

Sweat the small stuff first, and eventually you'll get to the bigger issues. We all want to see the other side of change right away: if we've lost our job, we're hoping for an amazing new career opportunity where we make a lot more money; if we've been dumped, we're looking for the perfect new relationship; if we've experienced the death of a loved one, we're searching for a painless way to cope. But first we have to take care of those small things on our to-do list, the ones we keep postponing— donating old clothes to charity, paying bills, creating a photo album, updating our résumé. Life may be waiting to give us the next big change, but the minor details need to be taken care of beforehand.

☑ Take Action

Write down the areas of your life that feel out of control, where things are piling up and need to get done—work, finances, home, health, friends, family, and hobbies. You don't have to tackle all these areas and their tasks now. Just get them all out of your head and onto a piece of paper; this action alone will make you feel lighter, less overwhelmed, and free.

Now take a look at your list. What are the essentials? Be practical. What actions do you need to take sooner rather than later? What definitely needs to get done, and what can wait? Who can help?

When change comes, time seems to disappear. You get so busy that you don't have a second to focus on "all the other things." That's why it's so important to stay on top of them. For me it was things like clearing clutter, paying bills, giving away old clothes, getting organized, returning phone calls, clearing e-mails, and updating my address book—small stuff really, but stuff that gives me a sense of control over my life. When the little things are handled, the bigger ones don't seem so difficult to tackle. When you build your muscle with the small stuff first, your self-esteem rises and you are able to take on a little bit more.

Cut down what needs to be done into small pieces and stages. Don't put unrealistic timelines on things or take on too much too soon. Be gentle. Today, do one small thing or, if you can handle it, two things.

4. Make a Decision

In the first thirty days of change, you are confronted with chaos, lack of clarity, and too many choices. It is during this time that you may feel compelled to make decisions, to move on with your life. This starts the circle of doubt, where you ask, "What if I don't make the right decision?" This is completely natural. But first you need to accept that there is no perfect decision, no clear-cut right or wrong. Often you have to use your intuition to sense what *feels* right.

Chunk the decision into its smallest possible elements. For example, I recently was talking with a friend of mine who was considering a career change. He got very stuck on the question *What am I going to do with the rest of my life?* I encouraged him to see his big career decision in terms of a smaller chunk of time. He could, for example, ask himself, "What do I want to do for the next couple of years?" Careers change, jobs change; maybe an element or a person is not yet in your life, and that will impact your next professional move in a few years. It's futile to make these types of all-encompassing decisions. Often, that is the very reason they feel so heavy and difficult to make—because we are asking ourselves the wrong question and trying to make the wrong decision, or because the decision is just not yet ready to be made and we are forcing ourselves to come up with an answer.

It's normal to feel some sense of trepidation around a decision, positive or difficult. Even if you feel some fear about your decision, your body and emotions will find a way to support you through it, which will make the process a lot easier. For example, if you think you want to move to a new town, make the decision to do so—even if you are still slightly unsure—and be open to what shows up to help you make it happen. If you want to be in a loving, intimate relationship, make a decision that this will happen, and then align your focus, thoughts, and beliefs with this vision. Focus on what you want, not what you don't want.

Remember that the space and time *before* a decision are often much harder than what happens after the decision has been made. Announcing the decision to friends or colleagues will help keep you on track. Ask yourself, *Who must I tell?* And decisions take focus. Keep this new decision at the forefront of your mind—and heart—with notes, symbols, pictures, or anything else that places it front and center in your life.

My friend Brooks has an analogy he refers to as *the butcher knife versus the butter knife*. It goes something like this: When change comes and you have to make a decision, are you going to approach it with a butcher knife or a butter knife? The *butter knife* approach is to take things slowly, test the waters, and make sure not to hurt anyone's feelings. With this approach, we don't deal with the change sharply, clearly, or precisely. The *butcher knife* approach, however, is to face a change head-on, with clarity, power, and precision. Ask yourself: *Which knife am I using right now? Am I committed to changing something? Or am I still on the fence?*

5. Read and Write

Most people I have met can name a favorite book that helped them move through change. This is usually a book that has come to signify a personal victory over a particular moment in life. It can range from a novel to a short story, a self-help book, a memoir, or a religious text. Books help give us courage, strength, and perspective. The books we are touched by often show people overcoming adversity and despair despite their circumstances. They show different paths, solutions, and new roads to travel. Go to a bookstore, and browse through any book that you are drawn to, in any section. There is a great book waiting for you right now.

Writing is also a great tool when you feel alone. Writing things down has been proven to help healing and to get you through change quicker. Research has shown that when you write something down, the likelihood of your making that thing happen is much higher. I write every night. Journaling helps me capture the best of what the day was about, and when I get it down on paper, it gives closure to the day. Things don't drag on to the next morning.

> *Action is a great restorer and builder of confidence. Inaction is not only the result, but the cause, of fear. Perhaps the action you take will be successful; perhaps different action or adjustments will have to follow. But any action is better than no action at all.*
> *—Norman Vincent Peale*

I also love the freedom that writing gives me. I can express anything I am feeling without fear of judgment or criticism. And the simple action of getting it out of my head creates more space in my mind for other things. When my thoughts are on paper, it's like they are not mine anymore. My head is no longer filled with the problem I've been holding on to, and now there is room for solutions to manifest themselves. Often ideas and solutions pop out of the page—things I wouldn't have seen without getting my thoughts on paper. Even when we seek out help, going through change can often be a very private journey. It can be hard to relate to others and difficult to articulate our feelings. That's why writing can be such a helpful tool during change: it's intimate, anonymous, and liberating. You don't need to explain anything to anyone, and no one will give you an opinion. This is your space to write what you need to write. A time to grieve, a time to dream, a time to vent, and a time to focus.

6. Do Something for Someone Else

Taking time to put your situation to the side and to focus on somebody else is a powerful way to get back in touch with who you are and what you can give. When you stop obsessing about your own issues and problems and instead direct your energy to helping somebody else, you will find that you also have the strength to move through your own challenging change.

I know a woman who recently became a single mother. During this period she decided to help an elderly woman who lived across the street in her neighborhood with grocery shopping, meals, and general organizing. Even though her whole life required major reorganization now that her husband had walked out, and she had very little free time, she found that the most calming action she could take was to help someone else. She felt important and necessary. If she didn't show up, this older woman would be stuck. She got back in touch with what really matters—being kind, being loving, and helping someone out during the day.

You don't have to help a stranger. Make a list of your friends and loved ones, even your colleagues, and ask yourself: *What can I do for this person that would help them? What does he or she need?* Your help can be as simple as sending a card, making a phone call, mailing a clipping of an interesting magazine article, or finally taking the time to share a meal.

When her brother committed suicide, Rachel found that helping others was the best method of moving through her own pain. During the first, and hardest, day after her brother's death, she nurtured her family in the most basic yet essential way. "I remember the first day after his death, I focused on feeding my family. They hadn't eaten all day, and I started feeding them. It was the only thing I knew how to do," she says. "Being there for others has always helped me get out of my own way."

To move through change, it's essential to bust through the illusion that you are the only one experiencing pain or suffering. It is the gift of perspective. Yes, your job, health, or finances may be changing, but you also have a responsibility to show up in the world for your friends, family, and community. Be bigger than just your change. Someone else needs you.

I love this Chinese parable about action.

> If you want happiness for an hour—take a nap.
> If you want happiness for a day—go fishing.
> If you want happiness for a month—get married.
> If you want happiness for a year—inherit money.
> If you want happiness for a lifetime—help others.

7. Get Quiet

When we are meditating, planning, visualizing, grieving, or dreaming, it may seem like we're not doing much of anything, but, as with a seed that's been planted, there is a lot going on under the ground. The concept of meditation—or any form of getting quiet and looking within—is one of action, not inaction. You are very much doing something when you work to quiet your mind: you are putting your mind in the gym, training it to let go of the change demons and to become calm and quiet. For me, meditation is an action I try to engage every day. You can move into a quiet place in numerous ways. You can take a walk, have a nice meal, sit in candlelight, or watch kids playing. There are endless ways to access the peaceful part that we all have inside of us.

As I mentioned in chapter 7, there is no right or wrong way to meditate; it's not about how to sit, what to wear, or what to chant. Meditation is simply a decision to be still, to breathe deeply, to allow our thoughts and emotions to come up naturally, to allow everything to be as it is, without changing or resisting anything. We get quiet to observe what's going on inside of us as opposed to all that's happening outside of us—where we usually spend all of our time. Meditation brings clarity, answers, and inner peace. We realize we are still whole, complete, and unbroken, despite the change. It's a way of getting our inner strength back. Meditation can last five minutes or fifty-five. The act is what counts, not its length or intensity.

If you are unsure about what to do next, get quiet, and wait until the decision becomes clear. If a decision feels extremely difficult or confusing, take that as a sign that's it's not yet ready to be made; just like cake batter in the oven, it's not yet baked. It's important to become comfortable and familiar with the time in between a change and the next stage of life. We are all continually rushing to get back to a place that feels safe and certain. The period between can be torture for most of us. So we rush, jump to conclusions, make decisions based on limited information and often fear, and overrule our intuition. Finding the ability to just be and to do nothing takes enormous courage.

8. Bring Joy Back

During change, be sure to pursue some pleasurable activities, even though life may seem very dark right now. Choose outlets where you can learn, be creative, and do something you've never done before. Or choose something that will make you laugh. What have you always wanted to try? You can take a class in wine tasting, cooking, massage therapy, French, or creative writing. You can learn how to salsa dance, volunteer in a shelter or at your local church, or become a big brother or sister. Anything goes. Whatever you choose to do, make sure it's something you do on a regular basis. You will meet new people, and it will bring some routine into your life as well. If life is taking you through a change, take a road never traveled and see where it leads.

> *The way to get started is to quit talking and begin doing.*
> *— Walt Disney*

Catherine, upset about being single, found a dancing class that changed her perspective. She says it empowered her and took her out of her head. It was something she would never have dreamed of doing before. But by allowing herself to have fun, Catherine felt more capable of handling the not-so-fun stuff, too.

In these simple activities, wisdom comes. We realize that though things may be changing, we are still the same person. Think about that for a moment: everything that is you on the inside is still intact. All the important parts have remained untouched by this change.

Though taking action is key, it is not the only answer to moving through change. In fact, there is no one answer. I have friends who are obsessed with taking action. They don't want to sit and be with their thoughts or feelings. They are always on the move. If you are the type who usually takes action, devote ten to twenty minutes a day to sitting and meditating, writing in a journal, or getting more rest. On the other hand, if you are the type who is less action oriented, take a walk, go to the gym, or take care of the little things.

✔️ Take Action
Get into the Changing Room

What can you do right now to feel better? It can be something you've done before or something new that you're trying for the first time. If your higher self were given the microphone, what would it tell you to do?

Here are some examples of what a change optimist would do:

- Call someone (a friend, pastor, colleague, therapist, healer) who can help you through change.
- Write your current thoughts and emotions on a blank piece of paper or in a journal. They don't have to be intelligent or funny or even grammatically correct. They just have to be honest.
- Make a list of all the organizational things you need to do: clean out closets, return phone calls, organize finances, make a dentist appointment, and so on. Pick a few to do each week so you don't become overwhelmed.
- Practice some form of physical activity. Stroll, walk, run, swim, do yoga, sign up for a challenge like a 5k race, dance, bike, jump rope, hike, kick-box—anything just to get moving! (Through movement, eventually there will be a change tipping point, a time when you realize you have passed through the door of change.)

- Read some inspiring books; they're free at the library.
- Light a candle and burn some sage to clean out the old, negative energy in your space.
- Do something for someone else.

What actions helped you the last time you were moving through change? What do you need to do now to move through change? Write it down. And follow through.

Your Plan

Having a plan is a key component of moving through change successfully. Knowing first and foremost, *why* you need to change, what you want to change, where you want to end up, and what emotions you are sick of feeling all contribute to charting a course of action now.

A plan that will work should follow these guidelines:

It has a clear outcome. (You know what you want.)

It is achievable.

It has realistic timelines.

It is inspiring and gives you a compelling future.

You are optimistic about achieving the goals it outlines.

You are clear as to why it's important for you to succeed.

It involves doing some new things, learning, and growing,

You have help and support from others to get through it.

It is written down in a visible place so your brain can easily focus on it and keep you on track.

You are flexible about it, and you understand that things don't always work out the way you think they will.

It feels right.

You are radically clear why it is important for you to achieve it.

A man I met who lost his wife after forty-nine years of marriage made a courageous decision to put himself "back out there." He had grieved his loss for many months and figured it was time to meet someone else. He didn't really have a plan, so I invited him to establish a fun strategy that involved some new things. In a matter of days, George had a plan that would take him through the next six months. He would sign up at a few dating sites (at age seventy-nine!), attend some lectures in town, and even go to the gym. Those were the three main components of his plan, and they put a smile back on his face. The next few months unfolded, and after about a hundred meetings over coffee, a new trim body, and some inspiration, George met a lady. This lady was just right for him for the next phase of his life. Today, they are happily together.

You see, George was clear about what he wanted was hopeful and was willing to follow a plan to head in that direction.

☑ Take Action
Let's Make a Plan

1. Establish what it is you want that would help you love your life more. What changes have you always wanted to make? What changes must you now fully embrace and face?

2. Write down all the reasons *why* these changes are a "must," a priority. What will you gain if you follow through?

3. Find three things to do to help you move in the direction of your desired change. Be sure to add something you've never tried before, and follow the guidelines above.

4. Create a wall of change.

The Wall of Change

At home or at the office—or both—create a wall of change. (It can literally be a wall, or a pin board, or some other surface.) Here you can post visual elements of what you want or need to change and how you want to feel. Create the wall with your end goal in mind.

You can write out bold promises to yourself: *I am in great health. I am changing the way I speak to my parents. I am being more patient and kind. I am finding time to exercise at least three times a week. I am recognizing three things to be grateful about every night. I am telling the truth. I am accepting my new situation. I am becoming financially secure.* You can also include some of the new change tools you have acquired in reading this book. You can write out a positive question like "What am I learning from this change?" Remind yourself of the change guarantee. Copy the Change Manifesto in chapter 1.

You can also cut out inspiring magazine images that symbolize the change you want to make and post them on the wall. (Or cut out words or sentences that you connect to.) If your goal is to lose weight, you might find a photo of a fit, healthy man or woman jogging; and if you're hoping to save your marriage and keep your family together, you might find a shot of a happy family sharing a meal. You can also post photos of the people in your life whom you hope to include in your change—parents, kids, friends, or colleagues.

The wall of change helps the mind focus. The brain is always looking to do something, so assign it stuff. Take charge of the changes you want to see in your life. I have a wall of change for every area of my life—including my business, where every member of the team contributes to it regularly.

One final word: Celebrate your victories, your progress, the small and big steps. Reward yourself, acknowledge yourself, notice what you are doing right, and focus on what is great. Get into a routine of doing this. Schedule it.

Inspiring Others

Why take action? Why even bother? Here is one good reason: you are either a warning to other people or an example for them. You can be a warning of how not to handle a divorce, a diagnosis, or debt; or you can be an example. Life *always* gives you the chance to be a role model for someone who is watching. Everyone is on the hunt for good people and good examples, people who take the bad and turn it around, who reach deep inside themselves and take the higher path, who move through change and come out stronger, who not only talk about making a change or pursuing something bigger but actually go out, take action, and make it happen. Be one of those people. Make this change count for more than just yourself.

As you strive to be inspiring, to move through change with grace, you'll find that there are times when you need to be a hero. You need to do what a hero would do, say what a hero would say, and believe what a hero would believe. You don't feel like a hero? Well, most heroes don't feel heroic most of the time, either. Nevertheless, we never hear of a hero hiding out somewhere and waiting for things to settle down. Or of a hero ignoring the destiny right in front of him or her. Heroes are where the action is. They step out, and they mix it up—no matter how scary and unpredictable the situation they're in. They move forward like a warrior and are never paralyzed; they never delay in taking on what life asks of them. Still don't feel like a hero? Act as if you do: imagine yourself being victorious, being an inspiring example of someone who has come through against impossible odds.

All of us relate to heroes, because at least some of the heroic values lie in each of us. We would never hide and retreat if the change involved someone we loved; we would be out there fighting. This time, you don't need to be a hero for someone else; now is the time to be a hero for yourself. Take action today and remain radically optimistic!

The First 30 Days: What to Remember

1. Taking action is part of the foundation for getting through change. Start with small steps so you don't get overwhelmed.

2. Remember the SEED of change (sleep, eat, exercise, drink). Health always helps. Get enough sleep, eat well, exercise, drink lots of water, and then focus on what else you need to do.

3. Making a plan is a very valuable tool for change. Get clear on why you want to change, be optimistic about it, set up realistic timelines, and give life the space to work its magic.

The Next 30 Days
and Beyond

Radical Optimism, Possibility, and New Directions

Our worst mistake is underestimating ourselves. And underestimating life. It's time to give both a chance. Remove any limitations on who you are and what life should be, and watch what unfolds.

Each one of us is already good at certain change principles. As you look back at the nine principles, ask yourself which ones you are not practicing or perhaps are new to you.

Recently, I felt my views on change really tested when I was putting the finishing touches on this book. I was all set to work with a publishing house that, at the last moment, decided to change its editorial guidelines and not publish dozens of books, including mine: the firm was hesitant to work with any authors who deviated from its religious philosophy. With just thirty days before the book was supposed to go to print, the universe had thrown a serious change at me. I guess it wanted to make sure I had read my own book!

Well, I certainly went through feelings of shock, upset, and even anger. I felt unlucky, let down, and out of control because there was nothing I could do. Eventually, I got to a place where I knew I was strong enough to get through this change despite the initial craziness of it all. This wasn't the first—and it wouldn't be the last—unpredictable change that had come my way, so I accepted it for what it was. I understood that I couldn't change the circumstances. And I wasn't about to change the content of the book and compromise my views. This was what was real now, so I didn't resist it or fight it. I first took some time to connect with my trusted friends upstairs. I was angry at them for seeming to have let me down, but I asked them to show me what was next, to reveal the better choice that was around the corner. And I also moved through all of the disempowering emotions. Fear, blame, doubt, impatience—they all showed up for a while!

> *Not in his goals, but in his transitions man is great.*
> *—Ralph Waldo Emerson*

But through it all, I believed that there must be a gift in this for me. I believed that life knew better and that it was working on my behalf. I was sure something good would come from this change eventually—a better publisher, better timing for the debut of the book, a better book itself—now that I had time to include new content. During this change, I was very mindful of what I said to myself and to others about the situation I was going through. I noted the questions I asked myself and what I imagined for the future, but I also let myself be sad for a while about the unexpected turn of events. I reached out to a friend in publishing, to my life coach, and to my family, and, like a reliable team, they

The Promise to Change

Please promise yourself
No matter who or what you will become
No matter how unpredictable life is
No matter the growth you will experience
No matter the loneliness, pain, and sadness that will arise
No matter the fear, the questions, the disbelief
No matter the doubts, the resistance, and the impatience
No matter the surprises, the joy, and the pain
Always take change by the hand and welcome it
For
Change will bring strength
Change will bring faith
Change will bring new possibilities, new people, new paths
Change will bring self-esteem
Change will bring you what you are ultimately looking for
Always change
In change you will awaken
In change you will become wise
And in change you will finally be in partnership with life

Ariane

blew wind into my sails and reminded me that everything was going to be better than OK. Finally, I made myself go for a daily run, I wrote in my journal, and I posted my new goal on sticky notes.

I was led to a new publisher—the right publisher—in less than thirty days. I now see, completely, clearly, and beautifully, why this book needed a different home. Things worked out so well that I was even able to remain friends with the previous publisher. But what a journey: I write a book on change, and, just to shake things up a bit, life asks me to change publishers at the last minute! It's perfect, really.

Now is the time to begin looking at change differently—for the first thirty days and for the rest of your life. Live the change as it is unfolding; don't try to speed up the process. Be patient, and wait to see what life brings you. Remember, every change has its own timeline, and every person comes with a unique change résumé and change muscle.

The next time you find yourself trying to breeze through a change, be still, and let the process unfold and develop in the way it needs to. Be very patient with yourself when going through transitions; don't let your emotions or negative beliefs and assumptions take over. You will find that the initial hesitation, the "stuckness," and the sadness run their course and that one day they just go away. You don't know when that will happen—that's up to the universe to decide—but it always does happen. Remember that time you were so incredibly sad or worried? Do you know exactly when it ended? Not really. So just be patient: this period will transform. Keep in mind that something is being revealed to you; keep your eyes open.

You cannot see the steps you have already taken in the right direction. As long as you remain patient and allow the change to unfold naturally, your life will rearrange itself faster than you thought.

Old Mind-Set Versus Optimist's Mind-Set

A new change mind-set will give you a clearer view of what change actually is (and what it isn't), but there will always be parts of every change that are impossible to fully understand. The more you train your mind to be comfortable with the mystery of it all, the easier changes today and in the future will be for you.

The next time you are in a period of change or transition, you will be familiar with the emotions and feelings that may still come up.

- You may feel discomfort and pain.

- You may resist.

- You may experience the change demons: blame, doubt, fear, shame, guilt, and impatience.

- You may ask yourself disempowering questions like *Why me? Why am I such an idiot?*

- You may have negative beliefs that appear to be very real.

- You may describe things by using negative language.

- You may beat yourself up.

- You may compare your situation with that of others.

- You may hide out and feel alone.

- You may feel stuck.

- You may not necessarily know where to start or what decisions to make.

As you move through more and more changes, you will begin to know these things innately, and you will be able to start seeing them from a place outside of yourself, a place where you are more aware and conscious. From here you will be able to make intelligent decisions. You will know the following things:

You are much stronger and more resilient than you ever imagined.

You can accept the change and move with the flow of the river rather than against it.

There is something bigger going on here, whatever that may be.

There is a part of you that remains calm when everything around you is changing.

You can recognize your change demons as familiar friends, and you know how to move past them with positive emotions.

From any change, something good will come eventually.

Your beliefs can make change much easier.

There are people available to help if you just ask.

There are groups of people who are either going through the same change now or have gone through it before. (If you like, you can join them at first30days.com.)

That it helps to surround yourself with people who have the same mind-set and philosophy about life and about change.

Grieving can help.

The language and words you use and the questions you ask can make change easier.

You know that there are certain actions, such as physical exercise, writing, meditating, and doing something for others, that can really help during times of change.

You know that you are going to have to step up, raise your standards, and start changing the parts of your life that are no longer serving you.

You know that despite what might be happening, everything will eventually be OK.

You know that life is on your side and that you have to be open to seeing the positive in every situation.

You are ready to face the next thirty days and beyond with strength, wisdom, courage, and hope. You have a set of tools to take on any change and to move through it gracefully. And when you need to be reminded of your new mind-set, refer to the following credo of optimism:

> *Firmly believe this is a temporary situation.*
> *—Christopher Reeve*

The First 30 Days Mind-Set

The Credo of a Change Optimist

Principle 1: I have positive beliefs—about change, about life, and about myself.

Principle 2: I know that change will always bring something good into my life.

Principle 3: I know I am resilient, strong, and capable of getting through anything.

Principle 4: I know that my emotions, including the negative ones, are there as a guide and that I can replace them with more positive ones.

Principle 5: I know that the quicker I accept or choose change, the less the pain and hardship will be.

Principle 6: I use empowering questions and words, I think better thoughts, and I allow any and every feeling to come up and embrace it.

Principle 7: I know I am connected to something bigger—my soul, my spirit, my higher self.

Principle 8: I surround myself with people who can help and who have an optimistic mind-set, and I create an environment that supports change.

Principle 9: I take action. I have a plan, and I take care of myself.

I want to end—and in some ways start—this journey with you by sharing a Spanish story that I love, "The Parable of the Trapeze." A great friend of mine sent it to me when I was deep in change and facing many fears and doubts. Its magic has always stayed with me, and its late author, Danaan Parry, was certainly one of us—a change optimist. The parable is taken from Parry's *Warriors of the Heart.*

Sometimes I feel that my life is a series of trapezes. I find myself swinging on a trapeze, or during a few moments, I fling myself across the space that lies between trapezes.

Most of the time, I spend life holding onto the trapeze bar of the moment. I swing myself at a certain speed and I have the sensation that I control my life. I know the right questions and even some of the answers.

But sometimes when I am happily, or not so happily, swinging, I look ahead, and what is it that I see in the distance? I see another trapeze coming toward me. It is empty and I know, in that part of me that knows, that this trapeze has my name on it. It is my next step, my growth, life that is searching for me. From the bottom of my heart I know that to grow, I must let go of the old trapeze that I know so well, and grab onto the new one.

Every time that this happens to me I hope (no, I pray) to not have to let go of the old trapeze completely before grasping the new one. But in that place where I know, I know that I must let go of the old trapeze completely and, for a moment, cross space before being able to grab onto the new one.

I am always very afraid. It doesn't matter that in my previous flights between trapezes I have always been successful. I always fear failing, crashing against the rocks that I can't see at the bottomless chasm below. But I do it anyway. Perhaps this is the essence of what mystics call the faith experience. There is no guarantee, no safety net and no insurance policy but you do it anyway, because to continue holding onto the old trapeze just isn't one of the options anymore. So, during an eternity that can last a microsecond or a thousand lives, I rise above the dark emptiness of "the past gone by, the future not yet come." This is what is called a "transition." I have come to believe that true change occurs only in these transitions. I mean true change, not the pseudo change that only lasts until the next time the old buttons are pushed.

I have also come to realize that, in our culture, this transition zone is considered to be a "nothing," an empty non-place between places. Of course, the old trapeze was real and I hope the new one coming towards me will also be. But what about the emptiness between? Is it simply an empty space that should be crossed as fast and unconsciously as possible? NO!! This would be to lose a great opportunity. On occasions, I suspect that the transition zone is the only real thing and that the trapezes are illusions that we create to avoid the emptiness in which real change, real growth occurs. Whether or not this be true, what is certain is that the transition zones in our lives are incredibly rich. They should be honored, even savored. Yes, despite all the pain, the fear and the feelings of being out of control that may accompany (though not necessarily) transitions, these are still the most vivid, full of growth, passionate and expansive moments in our lives.

Our Journey Continues

God does not require us to succeed. He only requires that you try.

—Mother Teresa

Our journey together does not end here. Please come and visit us on the Web, at www.first30days.com. There you will find a community of people who are making changes in their lives and who are embracing and moving through all types of transitions. You will find experts, interviews, and inspirational stories of how other people are handling change. You will find thirty days of e-mail tips on dozens of life changes. We want to help you in very specific ways—whether it's the loss of a loved one, changing careers, a new relationship, a health diagnosis, or finding the courage to pursue a dream. Whatever change you are making or facing, please visit us.

Come share your story with us or ask a question. We are here to support you on your journey through change 24/7.

And as Oprah said in her recent article about first30days.com, "The journey of a thousand miles may start with a single step or a double click!"

With love and respect,

Ariane

Acknowledgments

This book is the culmination of many many people who have stood by me, blown wind in my sails, offered advice and suggestions, helped me, made me laugh, believed in me and have been committed to making sure this book and idea is brought to life. So, with much emotion, I want to say a huge thank you to:

My team around the book: Marisa Belger, my editorial partner; David Black, my agent; Lisa Sharkey, who saw the potential of this as a book; Cynthia DiTiberio, my editor; Suzanne Wickham, my publicist; and all the others at HarperOne who I know put their time and love into this manuscript.

The wonderful people who believed in the First 30 Days idea at some important stage in its development: Mum, Dad, my brothers Steve and Alex, Dick Parsons, Mamie Healey, Alexis du Roy, Scott English, David Dunham, and Pam Hendrickson.

My entire First 30 Days Team: Joe, Steve, Sarita, Tony, Andy, Bill, Dave, Michelle, Elizabeth, Kristin, Victoria, Arnulf, Ashley, Caren, Larry, Kellie, and Andrew.

And my investors, advisors and partners: You continue to build a fantastic company and brand that is helping change peoples lives.

My friends who have been there for me: Doris, Monty, Brooks, Joe, Aisling, Charlotte, Tina, Randy, Rhea, Daryl, David, Garth, Patrick,

Angi, Franca, Matt, Paul, Simon, Tony, Victoria, Christine, Rob, Colin, Estelle, Giada, Jessica, Jill, Michael, Catherine, Hillary, Rosario, Jen, Philip, Stanton, Gary, all my Robbins trainer friends, and too many more to write here.

All the people who I have interviewed and who have shared their changes with me, who let me ask them numerous questions and who helped me get clear on the principles in this book.

My teachers and the wise souls who have crossed my path: Wayne Dyer, Desiree Marin, Dominique De Backer, Carmen Grenier, Dr. Tim, Tony Robbins, David Morehouse, Maddalena Gualtieri, Marianne Williamson, Dr. Robert Arrese, Deepak Chopra, and the authors of the hundreds of books I have read: Each of you have added something important to my life and hence to this book.

And finally. God and all my "friends upstairs." Thank you for the guidance, inspiration and for being with me at all times.

I am deeply grateful to you all.

Thank you. Thank you. Thank you.

Recommended Reading

I'd like to share some books I've enjoyed while exploring the subject of change. Some of these are referenced within the book.

Bridges, William. *The Way of Transition.* Perseus Publishing, 2001.

Chodron, Pema. *When Things Fall Apart; Heart Advice for Difficult Times.* Shambhala, 2000.

Chopra, Deepak. *Seven Spiritual Laws of Success.* New World Library, 1994.

Dooley, Mike. *Notes from the Universe.* Totally Unique Thoughts. 2003.

Dyer, Wayne. *Change Your Thoughts, Change Your Life: Living the Wisdom of the Tao.* Hay House, 2007.

Hawkins, David R. *Power vs. Force: The Hidden Determinants of Human Behavior.* Hay House, 2002.

Hay, Louise L. *You Can Heal Your Life.* Hay House, 1999.

Hicks, Jerry & Esther. *Ask & It Is Given.* Hay House, 2004.

Katie, Byron. *Loving What Is: Four Questions That Can Change Your Life.* Harmony Books, 2002.

Mitchell, Stephen. *Tao Te Ching. A New English Version.* Harper Perennial Modern Classics, 2006.

Myss, Caroline. *Sacred Contracts: Awakening Your Divine Potential.* Harmony Books, 2003.

Peale, Norman Vincent. *The Power of Positive Thinking.* Fireside/Simon & Schuster, 2003.

Ruiz, Don Miguel. *The Four Agreements.* Amber-Allen Publishers, 1997.

Senge, Peter. *Presence: An Exploration of Profound Change in People, Organizations, and Society.* SoL Publishing, 2005.

Siegel, Bernie. *Love, Medicine, and Miracles.* Harper & Row, 1986.

Tolle, Eckhart. *The Power of Now.* New World Library, 2004.

Walsh, Neale Donald. *Conversations with God.* Putnam's Sons, 1995.

Williamson, Marianne. *The Gift of Change.* Harper San Francisco, 2006.

Zander, Benjamin. *The Art of Possibility.* Harvard Business School Press, 2000.

The First 30 Days Mind-Set

The Credo of a Change Optimist

Principle 1: I have positive beliefs—about change, about life, and about myself.

Principle 2: I know that change will always bring something good into my life.

Principle 3: I know I am resilient, strong, and capable of getting through anything.

Principle 4: I know that my emotions, including the negative ones, are there as a guide and that I can replace them with more positive ones.

Principle 5: I know that the quicker I accept or choose change, the less the pain and hardship will be.

Principle 6: I use empowering questions and words, I think better thoughts, and I allow any and every feeling to come up and embrace it.

Principle 7: I know I am connected to something bigger—my soul, my spirit, my higher self.

Principle 8: I surround myself with people who can help and who have an optimistic mind-set, and I create an environment that supports change.

Principle 9: I take action. I have a plan, and I take care of myself.

Love the Book? Visit the Web Site!

Whether you're starting a new job, getting married, getting divorced, switching to the Mac, or have decided to go green, you'll find the help you need by visiting us on the world wide web at *www.First30Days.com*.

- Getting Started
- Top 5 Things to Do
- Expert Advice
- Helpful Tips
- Q&A
- Shared Wisdom
- And a whole lot more!

Visit us on the world wide web today at www.First30Days.com